THE Fire IN THE Cloud

LENTEN MEDITATIONS

THE Fire
IN THE
Cloud

LENTEN MEDITATIONS

Daily Reflections on the Liturgical Texts

FRANCIS MARTIN

CHARIS

SERVANT PUBLICATIONS
ANN ARBOR, MICHIGAN

Charis Books is an imprint of Servant Publications especially designed to serve Roman Catholics.

Scripture quotations are from the author's own translation unless otherwise indicated. Verses marked RSV are from the Revised Standard Version of the Bible, copyrighted 1946, 1952, 1971 by the Division of Christian Education of the National Council of Churches of Christ in the USA. Used by permission. Those marked NAB are taken from the New American Bible.

Published by Servant Publications
P.O. Box 8617
Ann Arbor, Michigan 48107

Cover design by Eric Walljasper

01 02 03 10 9 8 7 6 5 4 3 2 1

Printed in the United States of America
ISBN 1-56955-264-9

Library of Congress Cataloging-in-Publication Data

Martin, Francis, 1930-
    The fire in the cloud : Lenten meditations : daily reflections on the liturgical texts / Francis Martin.
        p. cm.
    Includes bibliographical references.
    ISBN 1-56955-264-9 (alk. paper)
    1. Lent—Prayer-books and devotions—English. 2. Catholic Church—Prayer-books and devotions—English. 3. Bible—Meditations. 4. Catholic Church. Lectionary for Mass (U.S.) I. Title.
    BX2170.L4 M37 2001
    242' .34—dc21

                                                                    2001003613

CONTENTS

INTRODUCTION

Our Exodus

In the closing line of the Book of Exodus we are brought to understand more profoundly the mystery of the cloud and the fire that guided the Israelites. The fire, which was really the very glory of God himself, was hidden in the cloud. "The cloud of Yhwh was over the Dwelling by day, and fire was in it by night in the sight of all the children of Israel throughout all the stages of the their journey" (Ex 40:38). As they made their way through the desert, Israel was guided by the cloud, and it revealed its hidden glory in times of darkness.

The burning flame in the cloud is the Word of God burning within the Scriptures. The cloud always guides us, but it reveals its hidden splendor when other lights grow dim and we catch a glimpse of the true radiance of the Son of God: the glory of God shining on the face of Christ Jesus (see 2 Cor 4:6).

Though the whole life of the Church, a "pilgrim Church on earth," is under the sign of the Exodus, Lent is the time when this becomes more readily apparent. For it is then that, like Moses and Elijah at the Transfiguration, we speak with Jesus about his own exodus and join him in his journey to suffering and glory (see Lk 9:31). During Lent, day by day with all the Church, we try to draw close to him, and we ask him to open our minds to understand the Scriptures, as he did for his disciples after his resurrection (see Lk 24:45). We gather with the

Church, at least spiritually if we cannot come to the daily Eucharist, and listen to the liturgical readings when, as Vatican II has taught us, "it is still Christ proclaiming his Gospel" ("The Constitution on the Sacred Liturgy," 33). At this special time the Word of God is most able to show its inner fire, since the liturgy, the native home for the Scriptures, dims in our hearts and minds all the other lights that dazzle and distract us, and we can see the glory of God in the cloud.

The Purpose of This Book

I am writing this book as a help to understanding the inner rhythm of the biblical texts the Church gives to us as manna for our desert journey and as a luminous cloud guiding us into the heart of the mystery of the suffering and glory of the Son of Man. The plan is simple. For each day I will give the reference to the liturgical texts of the day, and then I will give a brief meditation on them, usually accenting one text or the other and giving a more protracted account of the Sunday readings. In the earlier chapters I have often included prayers at the end of the meditation; then, as we enter more profoundly into the Paschal Mystery, readers are invited to compose their own prayers. I urge the reader to take up this book along with the Scriptures so that, as far as possible, the biblical text is at the center of your attention. For the year 2002 the Sunday readings are those of Cycle A. These are the most ancient set of Lenten readings, and they are always used in the Rite of the Christian Initiation of Adults. As we hear them Sunday by Sunday, we too are to prepare ourselves to renew our baptismal commitment.

A word about the translation of the biblical texts. We are in the process of transition in the English-speaking world. I am writing these meditations in the latter months of the year 2000 and the early months of 2001. I have available the revised translation for the Sundays but not for the weekdays. That means that there may be a slight discrepancy between the wording of my meditations and that of the text you have, taken from the *New American Bible* (NAB). This should not be a distraction since, if I wish to explain a particular word, I will explain it on the basis of the original Hebrew or Greek of the biblical text. Also, longer quotes are either my own translation or that of the *Revised Standard Version* (RSV).

The Principal Themes of the Daily Lenten Liturgical Readings

In the "Dogmatic Constitution on Divine Revelation," 21, we read:

> The Church has always venerated the divine Scriptures just as she venerates the body of the Lord, since, especially in the sacred liturgy, she unceasingly receives and offers to the faithful the bread of life from the table both of God's word and of Christ's body.

We should take this description of the Church's attitude seriously. For two millennia the Church has considered Scripture, along with the Eucharist, to be "the bread of life." That means that the words of the sacred text are meant to nourish us in a very remarkable way. In his *Confessions*, St.

Augustine quotes these words of Our Lord, the Truth, as addressed to Augustine himself and to us: "You will not change me into yourself, as bodily food: you will be changed into me."[1] No one reading these words can help but think of the Eucharistic bread, and that is quite right. However, we must remember that Augustine is speaking of the divine truth in all its forms. As we receive the words of Scripture, which, as we have just seen, are also the Bread of Life, we must understand that their proper effect is to change us into the divine reality which these words mediate.

There is power in the Word of God. It is the power to transform us into Christ if we will yield to it. Such is the constant witness of the New Testament, which declares, "The word of the cross ... is the power of God" (1 Cor 1:18, RSV), and, "The word of truth, the Gospel ... is bearing fruit and growing" (Col 1:5-6, RSV). If we will let the Word of revelation have its way in our hearts, we will be changed. We will become more and more like Christ, not by our own efforts but by yielding to the power inherent in what the Word reveals, by coming close to the fire hidden in the cloud.

During Lent the Church uses the Scriptures to teach us principally about three things. First, we are taught how to live our Christian lives more authentically. Second, we are brought mysteriously into the soul of Jesus Christ as he faces his impending suffering and death. Third, we receive instruction in the very meaning of Jesus' death and resurrection and *are brought into contact with these realities.*

In this way, if we are catechumens, we are being prepared to be "baptized into his death" (Rom 6:3), to be "strengthened with power through his Spirit in the inner man" (Eph 3:16), and to be bound to the Body of Christ by sharing in the one bread and the one cup (see 1 Cor 10:16-17). If we are already part of the Church, we are being prepared to renew that commitment and to "gaze on the glory of the Lord, being transformed into the same image [of Christ] from glory to glory" (2 Cor 3:18).

It will help us now to look briefly at these three themes that characterize the readings in Lent.

How to Live in Christ

From the very first day of Lent we are given instruction on how to live the life given to us by the Holy Spirit as the fruit of the death and resurrection of Jesus. In the first reading on Ash Wednesday the prophet Joel teaches us the meaning of fasting and the effect that it can have on changing our hearts and the heart of a nation. The responsorial psalm, Psalm 51, teaches us how to pray a genuine prayer of repentance, while in the second reading, St. Paul reminds us of the fact that there are times and seasons in the Christian life: "Now is the day of salvation." These readings reveal a special moment in the life of the Church, a moment when the grace of repentance is readily available. Pope John Paul II touches on this mystery of time and the Church:

> In Jesus Christ, the Word made flesh, time becomes a dimension of God, who is himself eternal. With the coming of Christ here begin "the last days" (see Heb 1:2), the "last hour" (see 1 Jn 2:18), and the time of the Church, which will last until the parousia. From this relationship of God with time there arises the duty to sanctify time.[2]

The verse before the gospel continues to sound the note of urgency: "If today you hear the Lord's voice, harden not your hearts." Finally, in the gospel for Ash Wednesday Jesus himself teaches us how to observe the three basic acts of biblical piety: prayer, fasting, and almsgiving.

The theme of how we should be living as Christians will recur frequently during Lent, especially in the early part of the season. If we will let the energy of the Word of God have its way in our hearts, we will see profound changes in our lives.

The Paschal Mystery

The readings at the Eucharistic liturgy during Lent are meant to bring us to a contemplative understanding of the meaning of the Passion and Resurrection of Jesus, who is the Paschal Mystery. This is particularly true of the readings from the Gospel of John. These readings are the focus of the Church's constant meditation during the latter weeks of Lent. However, there are earlier intimations of the Paschal Mystery.

On Friday of the second week of Lent, for instance, the readings show salvation for the people coming through the betrayal of the innocent, first in type (the patriarch Joseph, who was betrayed by his brothers) and then in Jesus' prophetic parable (the son killed by the wicked tenant farmers). We see this theme manifested dramatically in the songs of the Suffering Servant, which are read during Holy Week.

Another dimension of the Paschal Mystery developed by the readings, both weekday and Sunday, is that of the Sacraments of Initiation. Present among us during Lent are those who are preparing for Baptism, and all of us are preparing to renew our baptismal promises. Baptism is completed by Confirmation and reaches its fulfillment in the Eucharist. As the *Catechism of the Catholic Church* (*CCC*, 1212), quoting Pope Paul VI, reminds us:

> The sharing in the divine nature given to men through the grace of Christ bears a certain likeness to the origin, development, and nourishing of natural life. The faithful are born anew by Baptism, strengthened by the sacrament of Confirmation, and receive in the Eucharist the food of eternal life.

Most of the liturgical readings of this type teach us about Baptism, "the basis of the whole Christian life, the gateway to life in the Spirit, and the door which gives access to the other sacraments" (*CCC*, 1213). Thus, we will read about Naaman's healing by means of what seemed to be ordinary water but was in fact rendered powerful by the prophetic word through Elisha (2 Kgs 5:1-15; Monday of the third week). We will read of the water flowing from the renewed temple and forming a life-giving and healing river. We see the man at the pool of Bethesda healed by Jesus' word as he waits for the waters to stir (Ez 47:1-12; Jn 5:1-16; Tuesday of the fourth week). As we will see, the whole of the Paschal Mystery is given to us in the Sunday liturgies, which structure the whole of the Lenten period.

The Interior Life of Jesus

It has been given to many saints and mystics to enter mysteriously into the heart of Jesus, to experience the love that is there, and to know for themselves what Jesus suffered interiorly as he approached his passion and death. In the Lenten liturgy the Church enters into this mysterious place, the fire in the cloud. We do so mostly through hearing the Word of God as it comes forth from two sources: from those psalmists who were among, and who spoke for, all the suffering poor men of Israel; and from Jeremiah, whose whole life was a prophecy of Jesus, the Suffering Servant.

These texts are a sacrament: they express an anticipated participation in the sufferings of Jesus the Messiah, and they are as well texts and prayers that have passed through the soul of Jesus himself. If our hearts are open, as these texts are read in the liturgy, this inner mystery of Jesus will touch us and enable us to love him more completely.

The Structuring of Lent Through the Sunday Readings

The Sunday readings in the liturgy follow a three-year cycle: "A," "B," and "C." For the year 2002 we have cycle A, which represents the ancient, closely crafted series of Sunday readings designed to prepare the catechumens for Baptism. We will study these texts at length during the course of these meditations. Here it is important to note that it is the whole Church that is preparing for the grace of Baptism.

First, we carry in our hearts, each one of us, the whole body of catechumens throughout the world: they are being prepared by the Holy Spirit to be "baptized into one Body" and "given to drink of one Spirit" (1 Cor 12:13)—that is, to be one with us in Christ. Second, Lent is for the whole Church a time of spiritual enlightenment and of a deeper, purer relationship with the Trinity. The movement of the Church through Lent to Easter and then beyond to Pentecost is, at its depths, the movement of the Holy Spirit, who uses the liturgy with its readings, prayers, music, and sacraments as a means of freeing us from sin and conforming us to Christ.

In our meditations we will be centering on the readings; it is these, particularly the Sunday readings, that structure the movement of Lent and give to each Sunday its special tone and grace. In Cycle A the accent is on the preparation of the catechumens. This is so true that, at the Mass the catechumens attend, these readings are used even during Cycles B and C. The meditations on these Sundays are in chapters eight and nine respectively.

The first Sunday of Cycle A deals with the mystery of sin, which was introduced into history by our first parents (first reading), healed by the power of Christ, the new Adam (second reading), who is then held up to us as our model in times of temptation (gospel). The second Sunday puts us in touch with God's call on our lives, using the example of Abraham (first reading), describing our own call (second reading), and finally turning our gaze to Jesus transformed on Mount Tabor (gospel). The next three Sundays mark a progression in themes: the gift of God as living water, the work of God as enlightenment, and the power of God to give us a life greater than death.

We then arrive at Palm Sunday, and at this point the cycles basically converge to celebrate Holy Week and the Feast of the

Resurrection. We have arrived at the heart of the Paschal Mystery, into which the catechumens are baptized and by which they are nourished at the Eucharist. In the same way, we who have already been purified by the action of the Holy Spirit are identified more intimately with the same mystery: "The Christ in you, the hope of glory" (Col 1:27, RSV).

The Mysteries of the Life of Christ

We read in the Book of Revelation: "And I saw in the midst of the throne and the four living beings, and in the midst of the elders, *a lamb standing as having been slain,* having seven horns and seven eyes which are the seven spirits of God sent into all the earth" (Rv 5:6). Jesus, the Lamb still bearing the marks of his slaughter, is now endowed with divine power and knowledge. His earthly experiences have made of his humanity, now transformed at the Resurrection, a multifaceted source of grace for those who turn to him in faith. These events through which Jesus lived, what tradition calls the "mysteries of the life of Christ," are, each in its own way, a source of particular blessing and grace for those who touch them. As St. Leo once eloquently expressed it:

All those things which the Son of God both *did and taught* for the reconciliation of the world, we not only know in the account of things now past, but we also experience in the power of works which are present.[3]

The source of the power that we experience when we come into contact with what Jesus "did and taught" is the transformed humanity of Jesus Christ. Thus, the Letter to the Hebrews tells us: "We do not have a high priest unable to share by experience our weaknesses, [but one] having been tested in all ways, because he is like us, [however] without sin" (Heb 4:15). He is fixed in that act of love in which he died, and thus exists forever as the tried and tested one.

It is precisely because of this that the exhortation is given to us: "Let us approach, then, with assurance the throne of grace that we might receive mercy and find grace at the right time of need" (Heb 4:15-16). Not only will we receive a compassionate reception, but also Jesus, having learned obedience from what he suffered, has become "the source of eternal salvation to all who obey him" (Heb 5:9, RSV). The High Priest whom we are urged to approach has not only shared our temptations and overcome them, but he still bears his wounds and forever retains the effects of his passage among us. In his now glorious humanity, he is the source and the cause of our salvation: power goes out from him (see Lk 6:19; 8:46).

Jesus is the source of divine life because his sacred humanity is joined to the very Person of the Word of God. The transformed humanity of Christ—his mind, will, emotions, memory, as well as his body—is now perfectly apt to be the instrument of his divinity. It confers a special grace on the believer in keeping with that event of his earthly life that the Church, or each person, turns to in faith. A famous medieval monk, Rupert of Deutz, exhorts us to penetrate into the inner wellsprings of Jesus, who lives now still bearing within him the actions he performed on earth: "What he did then, let us listen to now, and in his external action let us make out the mystery."[4]

The early Fathers of the Church paid close attention to the biblical text, but what they spoke about, under the guidance of the text, was the recounted event as it still lives on in the transformed sacred humanity of the Son of God. Taking their inspiration from what the gospel writers had done, and in dependence upon their authoritative presentation, the Fathers endeavored to bring their audience into a life-giving contact with Jesus. It is this contact with Jesus, as he lives now with that particular aspect of earthly life, that is able to touch us in a special way: what the Fathers called the "power of the mystery."

I would like to quote here some lines taken from a work by Dom Columba Marmion that was very instrumental in restoring an understanding of the mysteries of Christ's life to the Church. They may serve as a fitting conclusion to this brief Introduction and prepare us to meditate on the Lenten readings:

> For although it is always the same Saviour, the same Jesus, pursuing the same work of our sanctification, each mystery, however, is a fresh manifestation of Christ for us; each has its special beauty, its particular splendour, as likewise its own grace.... Each of Christ's mysteries, representing a state of the Sacred Humanity, thus brings to us a special participation in His divinity.[5]

CHAPTER ONE

The First Four Days
The Inner Life

Sometime in the sixth century, out of a desire to have a full forty-day Lent, and since the Sundays are not considered fast days, the four days preceding the first Sunday were added. They are important in our understanding of the whole season, particularly in regard to the first theme, our life in Christ. We will consider the readings of each of these days in turn.

❧

Ash Wednesday
Joel 2:12-18; 2 Corinthians 5:20–6:2; Matthew 6:1-6, 16-18

On this very first day we are presented with two fundamental aspects of Lent: community and interiority. Our Lord's words in the gospel bring these themes together in a profound way. Jesus is talking about the three fundamental acts of biblical spirituality: prayer, fasting, and almsgiving. We pray and ground our very life in this interaction with God the Father; we fast from those things that protect us from experiencing our weakness and need for God; and we give alms from the surplus that we thus achieve so that others may have what they need. St. Matthew has arranged this threefold aspect of biblical spirituality so that prayer is at the center. This sets the Our Father (which follows in his gospel text at this point) at the very pinnacle of the whole Sermon on the Mount.

In his teaching Our Lord draws a contrast between "hypocrisy" and a single-hearted desire to please the Father. Hypocrisy is an individualistic warping of the very meaning of prayer, fasting, and almsgiving. And at the same time it is a lie, since such gestures do not express the genuine desire of the human heart to be in union with God, to be restrained in serving oneself, and to be of service to others. Hypocrites are seeking only human recognition. The tragedy here is that the misled approval they obtain is all that they achieve: "They have received their reward."

The marvel put forward in Jesus' teaching, and made real by his death and resurrection, is the reality of the Father and of his love for each human being he has made. Now, because of the revelation brought about by Jesus, we can know the Father and love him, confident that he sees what we do in secret and receives it in love. Nothing escapes his deep, attentive gaze, and his heart forgets nothing. St. Thérèse of Lisieux once said that sometimes she wished that the Father were not all-knowing because she would love to do something for him in such a way that he did not know it was done by Thérèse.

A pure desire to please the Father and the confidence that he knows our hearts lie at the source of the saints' actions. By teaching us this possibility—and Matthew is insisting on this—Jesus is making known to us the true source of our greatness, while pointing to the fact that this new interiority makes possible a union with others that goes beyond our human resources. It is, in fact, the twofold experience of the Father as "my Father" and "our Father."

This mystery is set forth for us in "Pastoral Constitution on the Church in the Modern World." This Vatican II document teaches us, first, that it is only in the revelation of the Father and his love that we can understand ourselves. Then, it is only by going out of ourselves and imitating the mutual self-gift of the Trinity that we can find ourselves. Let us look at two key texts in that document where this teaching is set forth.

The truth is that only in the mystery of the incarnate Word does the mystery of man take on light. For Adam, the first man, was a figure of Him Who was to come, namely Christ the Lord. *Christ, the final Adam, by the revelation of the mystery of the Father and His love, fully reveals man to man himself and makes his supreme calling clear....* (22).

Indeed, the Lord Jesus, when He prayed to the Father, "that all may be one ... as we are one" (Jn 17:21-22) opened up vistas closed to human reason, for he implied a certain likeness between the union of the divine Persons, and the unity of God's sons in truth and charity. *This likeness reveals that man, who is the only creature on earth which God willed for itself, cannot fully find himself except through a sincere gift of himself* (24).

Prayer:

We want to thank you, Lord, for showing us, through the Church's breaking of the bread for us, the meaning of Lent from the very first day. We ask you to make us faithful to prayer, fasting, and alms-giving so that we can imitate you as dear children, walking in love as Christ walked in love and gave himself up for us. May our lives be directed to you, and may you see in secret and be pleased. Amen.

Thursday After Ash Wednesday
Deuteronomy 30:15-20; Luke 9:22-25

Today we hear the call to make a decision. Are we going to follow Jesus? The first reading is from the Book of Deuteronomy, a work composed by a great saint and mystic who reedits and sums up the first four books of the Law (*Deuteronomy* means "second law"). He uses ancient material and presents Moses preaching God's will to the people. The section we have today forms part of the conclusion. Here the Lord is preaching to us: "See, I have placed before you life and good, death and evil." Life is in keeping his commandments; death is in turning away. This is no arbitrary imposition of a will foreign to us, but rather it is the instruction of one who loves us and who is teaching us the way to happiness.

Once God the Father said to someone, "Up to now you have been obedient enough, but you often do my will while really wanting to do something else. Now I am going to work in your heart so that you will love my will and find delight in it, even if you suffer. Your delight will be to prefer what I prefer, because you will love me and nothing will seem more important than my will."

This promise is held out to all of us and is ours if we welcome it. St. Paul teaches us as much when he says: "Therefore, my beloved, as you have always obeyed, so now, not only as in my presence but much more in my absence, work out your own salvation with fear and trembling; for God is at work in you, both to will and to work for his good pleasure" (Phil 2:12-13, RSV).

The choice set before us in the gospel steps from the shadows of a general obedience to God to a clear following of Jesus Christ. For the first time we meet the theme to be developed throughout Lent, the mystery of the suffering and glory of the Son of Man. He is to "suffer greatly" and to be rejected by the leaders of the people he has come to save. He will be killed and on the third day be raised.

Take time to gaze with the eyes of your heart into this abyss of light. Seek to understand the wisdom of God, who has responded to our darkness and sin by sending his Son to enter into our pain and, in solidarity with us, to die in an act of love and thus bear all of us with him back to the Father. This is the meaning of the prophecy that Jesus delivers in today's text.

But there is more. We are not spectators of this mystery; we are a part of it. Jesus tells us that if anyone wishes to come after him, that person must deny himself, take up his cross daily, and follow Jesus. We have the privilege of being conformed to him: "For it has been granted to you that for the sake of Christ you should not only believe in him but also suffer for his sake" (Phil 1:29, RSV).

Only the saints can tell us the joy that lies hidden in this union with Jesus. We must not be afraid of this call. Our Lord tells us that whoever wishes to save his life will lose it, while the one who loses his life for Jesus' sake will save it. A new Moses, he is setting before us life and good, death and evil. But now embracing the will of God and rejoicing in his life stem from a deep and personal knowledge of Jesus and a love for him, given to us by the Holy Spirit. This love enables us to embrace the difficulties of our life, knowing these are not the accidents of a world out of control but are the personal will of the Father for us. This Father is leading us to an eternal union with himself in Christ Jesus.

Prayer:

Father, thank you for the care you take of us. Thank you that our lives are not trivial but meaningful to you, for whom everything genuinely human is precious. We are proud that you are at work in us, realizing your good purpose. We pray for all those who, at this moment, need your special help in the difficulties of their lives. We pray for the poor and the sick, for single mothers left to care for their children, for those in prison or bondage who yearn for freedom. And by your mercy, we choose you and we choose life. Amen.

Friday After Ash Wednesday
Isaiah 58:1-9; Matthew 9:14-15

Today's readings bring us deeper into the mystery of fasting and mourning. They teach us that self-denial means principally caring for others out of our own resources. The Lord himself describes the fast that he expects from us: releasing unjust bonds, taking the yoke of poverty from people, setting the oppressed free, sharing our food with the hungry, clothing those who are without clothes, giving a home to the homeless, and caring for our own families. The Lord promises us that, if we do these things, when we ourselves cry out for help he will say to us, "Here I am!"

The first step in responding to this text is to repent as a Church for the ways we have not obeyed the Lord. On March 19, 2000, Pope John Paul II led the Church in a penitential rite in which, among other things, we repented for our lack of care for the poor: precisely, for not fasting as the text from Isaiah tells us to. Let us repeat that prayer now.

A Representative of the Roman Curia: Let us pray for all the men and women of the world, especially for minors who are victims of abuse, for the poor, the alienated, the disadvantaged; let us pray for those who are most defenseless, the unborn killed in their mother's womb or even exploited for experimental purposes by those who abuse the promise of biotechnology and distort the aims of science.

The Holy Father: God, our Father, you always hear the cry of the poor. How many times have Christians themselves not recognized you in the hungry, the thirsty, and the naked, in the persecuted, the imprisoned, and in those incapable of defending themselves, especially in the first stages of life. For all those who have committed acts of injustice by trusting in wealth and power and showing contempt for the "little ones" who are so dear to you, we ask your forgiveness: have mercy on us and accept our repentance. We ask this through Christ our Lord. Amen.

The second step in responding to this word of the Lord is to put it into practice and to teach our children to do the same. During this Lent find ways of alleviating the suffering of those whose lives touch your own. Give to the poor, visit the sick and lonely, see what you can do to help those who are homeless and depressed, look someone in the eye (you will see Christ) and offer your love in a concrete and practical way. Then, as the Lord promises us, our own light will shine and our own wounds will be healed.

Once a woman religious very sick from cancer was praying with a group of her friends and asking the Lord for healing. Someone in the group said to her: "Sister, have you released everyone in your life from the bondage of your own unforgiveness?"

The answer was no, not everyone. In fact, she felt great rancor toward her own superior. With the help of those praying with her, the sick woman forgave her superior. Some weeks later the doctors declared her free of cancer. "Then your light will shine like the dawn, and your wound will quickly be healed" (Is 58:8).

In the gospel Jesus teaches us both about fasting and about himself. When questioned why his own disciples did not fast, he replied that they were, at that time, present at a wedding. A time would come when the bridegroom would be taken away from them; then they would fast. This proverb is an indirect revelation of Jesus as the Bridegroom of God's people, and therefore the one who, in God's role, espouses the people.

We Christians are now in the mysterious time when the bridegroom is both with us and not with us. He is here—in his Church, in the sacraments, in his Word, in his members, and in a special way in the poor. And he is yet to come and reveal all the glorious fruit of his death for us. In the meantime, we can rejoice with him and still suffer with him. We can know the blessedness of those who mourn, yearning for the completion of Christ's work, when every tear will be wiped away, and there will be no need for fasting in solidarity with those who do not have what they need.

Prayer:
Blessed Jesus, Son of God, teach us to share in your love and to fast from all that perpetuates our illusion of self-sufficiency. Amen.

Saturday After Ash Wednesday
Isaiah 58:9-14; Luke 5:27-32

Today we continue to hear the Lord's instruction about fasting from the same chapter of the Book of Isaiah that we heard yesterday. We are told two things. The first of these, as in the earlier portion of the text, is care for those who are in need. God tells us to take oppression out of our society, to refrain from speech that destroys others, to feed the poor and needy, and to care for the afflicted.

How do we react to this word from the Lord? We should first repent for the ways we have not cared for those who are in greater need than we are.

The story is told of a woman who was starving along with her child. She went to Mother Teresa, who gave her the last bowl of rice in the house. The woman took the rice, divided it in two, and gave half to another woman who was in equal need with her child. She will hear from the Lord one day: "Come, blessed of my Father, I was starving along with my child, and you divided your pittance with me to save us from starving."

Once again let us return to the Liturgy of Repentance led by Pope John Paul II. Let us join him in praying, in the name of the whole Church, for the way we have pretended to fast but not in a manner prescribed by the Lord.

Representative of the Roman Curia: Let us pray, that contemplating Jesus, our Lord and our Peace, Christians will be able to repent of the words and attitudes caused by pride, by hatred, by the desire to dominate others, by enmity towards members of other religions and towards the weakest groups in society, such as immigrants and the homeless.

The Holy Father: Lord of the world, Father of all, through your Son you asked us to love our enemies, to do good to those who hate us and to pray for those who persecute us. Yet Christians have often denied the Gospel; yielding to a mentality of power, they have violated the rights of ethnic groups and peoples, and shown contempt for their cultures and religious traditions: be patient and merciful towards us, and grant us your forgiveness! We ask this through Christ our Lord.

Should we not gather together and acknowledge our sins as a Church? Should we not admit that God's name is dishonored in this world mostly because we, who have been privileged to bear that name, have been such poor witnesses to the Good News of the transforming power of the cross of Christ? Should we not, each one of us, acknowledge that our sins have pulled down the holiness of the Church? Is it not with this attitude that we can go to the sacrament of Reconciliation and be reconciled to God and to the Body of Christ and thus, in the power of Christ, repair the damage we have done to all those who are joined to us in this Body?

The gospel text contains once again an indirect self-revelation on the part of Jesus, this time as well in the form of a proverb. Jesus was at a party being thrown by Levi, the tax collector, to celebrate his call by Jesus. The Pharisees and scribes were shocked by his presence, to which Jesus replied, "The healthy do not need a doctor, the sick do." Had they wished to reflect on this answer, his opponents would have understood that, once again, Jesus was describing himself in terms that were used by God himself in the Book of Exodus: "I, Yhwh, am your healer" (Ex 15:26).

Prayer:

Jesus, thank you for teaching us what it means to fast and for giving us the courage we need to come to you. You came to heal us, and we come to you for that spiritual and physical healing that reveal your compassion and your power. Look upon the whole world, and let all hear you call them to celebrate with you the saving work you accomplished in obedience to your Father. Amen.

CHAPTER TWO

The First Week of Lent
Pursuing Holiness

As we have already had occasion to see, the Sunday liturgies during Lent provide a basic direction and structure to the season. This means that there are three slightly different tones to Lent depending upon which cycle is being used. As we have also noted, the first cycle, Cycle A, is the oldest and the one most attuned to the formation of the catechumens and candidates for their baptism and reception into the Church. That is why these readings are always used at the liturgy that the catechumens attend, no matter what cycle is being observed.

We will consider the readings of Cycle A here in the main part of the book. The meditations on the readings of Cycles B and C for the first five Sundays of Lent are in chapters eight and nine. The daily readings are the same in all three cycles, and the liturgy of Palm Sunday can be treated as one, despite the variations in the gospel readings.

Sunday of the First Week
Genesis 2:7-9, 3:1-7; Romans 5:12-19; Matthew 4:1-11

Let us place ourselves with the catechumens as they begin the last part of their journey to baptism. These texts, which are solemn, are meant to help them, and us, discover the true source of the darkness and distortions of our existence and the marvel of the solution provided by God. At the Easter Vigil, just after the catechumens are baptized, we will be called upon to renew our own faith and our baptismal commitment to Jesus Christ.

The first reading shows us the nature of sin. Sin is not some cosmic catastrophe; it is unfaithfulness to a covenant. God planted a garden for Adam's delight; the place where God and humanity meet must be beautiful. After giving him all the fruit of the trees as his own, God gave a command to Adam: "Of all the trees of the garden, eat as you will, but of the tree of the knowledge of good and evil, do not eat, for on the day you eat of it, you will certainly die" (Gn 2:16-17).

By giving this command, God gave Adam the opportunity to trust him and obey, not out of fear or coercion but out of love. Adam was to respond in gratitude for all that God had done. The inspired sage who wrote this text modeled his account of this relationship on that which existed between Yhwh and Israel.

The serpent was the most cunning of all the beasts that the Lord God had made. He was made by God and under God's authority, yet he managed to convince the woman of an utterly unverifiable hypothesis: that God was jealously holding back something that would lead her and Adam to independence and power. The serpent said to the woman, "God knows that on the day you eat of this fruit your eyes will be opened, and you will be like gods, knowing good and evil." That is, you can do what you want, and *you* will declare whether it is good or evil.

Adam and Eve fell into the trap. From a pure and unveiled communication with each other ("They were naked and unashamed"), they came to know shame, and their communion was broken. Then they experienced the second effect of sin: they knew fear and hid themselves from God. By turning from God, they lost authority over their own lives, they broke their intimacy with each other, and they lost union with God. This state of antagonism, characteristic of human relating, is epitomized in the tension between man and woman: "For your husband shall your longing be, and he will lord it over you" (Gn 3:16). Now we see domination as well as connivance in domination enter: the lie of power and the lie of powerlessness. Who can deliver us from this incessant twisting of human relationships?

The second reading provides the answer. By his love, trust, and submission to the Father—even unto death—Jesus, the obedient one, restores our relationship to the Father and brings us back to life. "So then, as through one transgression there was condemnation for all, so too, through one just act there was justification which is life for all. For, just as through the disobedience of the one man, the many were constituted sinners, so too through the obedience of the one, the many will be constituted just" (Rom 5:18-19). Jesus also makes it possible for us to relate to each other, and he makes his own love for the Church the source and model for the restored relationship between man and woman, husband and wife.

Finally, in today's gospel we are given a glimpse of the victory over Satan and evil that Jesus will win by his tenacious fidelity to the will of the Father. The Church must be faithful to the Father's will for her by not relying excessively upon human devices to accomplish divine goals. This is in accordance with Jesus' own example of fidelity to the Father's will, even as he was tempted by Satan to be a Messiah other than the one willed by the Father, to be a Messiah who would perform spectacular works that would force a superficial allegiance.

The Lord in his glory now not only teaches us how to deal with the inevitable fact of the solicitation to evil, but he is the very source of grace that strengthens us and gives us a share in his victory. "For we do not have a high priest unable to know by experience our weaknesses, having been tempted in all ways, in keeping with his likeness to us, without sin. Let us approach, then, with assurance the throne of grace that we might receive mercy and find grace at the right time of need" (Heb 4:15-16).

Prayer:

Blessed are you, God and Father of Our Lord Jesus Christ. You have saved us from the destitution our sin has brought into the world, and you have healed us by the stripes your Son bore for us. As we begin our Lenten journey keep us alert, cautious as well as trusting, and optimistic in our struggle with evil. Amen.

Monday of the First Week
Leviticus 19:1-2, 11-18; Matthew 25:31-46

In keeping with the early Lenten themes, the readings continue to instruct us on how we should live as Christians. The texts today speak of how seriously God looks upon the way we relate to one another.

The first text is part of what is called the Holiness Code in the Book of Leviticus. Here is the reason for acting as God prescribes: "You will be holy because I, Yhwh your God, am holy." That is, "By acting this way you remove yourselves from the realm of darkness and sin and make room for my presence among you so that I can bring you into union with me in the realm of light and life."

The section of the text we have today is concerned exclusively with interpersonal relations, yet at the end of every short series of commandments we find the phrase, "I am Yhwh." The Lord himself is the norm for the way we relate to each other: we should act as he does. He is also the one who rewards and punishes us on the basis of how we treat each other. We can read in a later text in the Book of Proverbs (19:17, RSV) this same principle of identification: "He who is kind to the poor lends to the Lord, and he will repay him for his deed." The last line of our reading here sums it all up: "You shall love your neighbor as yourself. I am Yhwh" (Lv 19:18, RSV).

The gospel reading continues this same principle, but now God has come to dwell among us. Indeed, one among us is actually the Son of God, equal to the Father. From now on the norm for our acting and the consequences of our relating, for good or ill, are measured by the fact that Christ is identified with every human being and in a special way with those who are joined to him. Jesus responded to Paul, who was on his way to persecute the Church in Damascus, "I am Jesus, whom you are persecuting" (Acts 9:5, RSV).

It is also important to note the parallel between several of those actions towards the poor, which Jesus describes as being done to him, and the deeds the Lord lists in last Friday's reading. It is precisely from this correlation of deeds and actions that we hear the true meaning of fasting: "I was hungry and you gave me food,... a stranger and you welcomed me, I was naked and you clothed me" (Mt 25:35, RSV; Is 58:7). Here we see how deeply personal—that is, other-directed—our commitment to the Lord must be. The difference between mercy and pity is that mercy looks to the person and pity looks to the need. We are called upon to practice mercy, that is, to look to the other *person* and love him, seeing Christ in him and imitating the love that our Lord Jesus Christ has shown to us. As an ancient Christian saying has it, "When you see your brother, you see the Lord your God."

Such an understanding of the intimate identity of Christ and one's neighbor in no way detracts from the need for a deep, personal, and experiential relationship to Christ himself, one that only prayer can yield in its fullness. It does point, however, to the fact that love for God and love for our neighbor are so closely intertwined that each supports the other and acts as the criterion of the other's authenticity. St. Augustine goes so far as to say that as we love our neighbor we give greater sway to the love that God has for both our neighbor and ourselves. This is the way to a mystical knowledge of

God: "Love your neighbor, then look within yourself at the source of this love. There you will see, as far as you are able, God" (*Commentary on John's Gospel* 17, 8). In another place he explains why this is so: "Let him love his brother, and he will love the same love. For he knows the love with which he loves, more than the brother whom he loves. So now he can know God more than he knows his brother: clearly known more, because more present; known more, because more within him; known more, because more certain" (*On the Trinity* VIII, 8, 12).

Prayer:

Jesus, open up the eyes of our hearts that we may see reality as it is, that we may see you in all those whose lives touch ours, especially in our own families and those who are poor and in any need. Thank you for the privilege of loving and serving you in each other. Amen.

⚜

Tuesday of the First Week
Isaiah 55:10-11; Matthew 6:7-15

Today we are initiated into the deep dynamic of prayer. We see that all prayer really begins with God and returns to God, in and through a willing heart. As the *Catechism of the Catholic Church* (2565) teaches, "Christian prayer is a covenant relationship between God and man in Christ. It is the action of God and of man, springing forth from both the Holy Spirit and ourselves, wholly directed to the Father, in union with the human will of the Son of God made man."

The first reading tells us that God's Word—his plan and his action in this world—is like rain. It always produces the effect for which it has come to earth. Rain makes the earth fertile, and God's will makes the human heart fertile. The difference is that the earth will respond spontaneously, while we must freely yield to the action of God, which is to produce its fruit in us. Our hearts must be, as the *Catechism* expresses it, "in union with the human will of the Son of God made man."

The prayer that Jesus gave us is a perfect illustration of the principle that prayer is "the action of God and of man, springing forth from both the Holy Spirit and ourselves." In the human heart of Jesus lay a fire of love and intimate, tender desire for the will of the Father. The prayer that he taught us expresses the movements of his own heart. The movement of the Holy Spirit entered first like rain into his heart, and from there this action returned to the Father. This movement was of such intensity that when it was fulfilled in the act of love in which he died and rose, the whole human race was enabled to enter into this prayer.

From our hearts, too, can come this intimate expression, which is that of Christ, Head and members. The whole secret of prayer, indeed the whole secret of life, is to yield to the action of the Holy Spirit, who is always moving in us to form us into the likeness of Christ. That is why Paul can say that the quintessential activity of the Spirit is to reveal the face of the Father of Our Lord Jesus Christ. This revelation thus produces in us a divine affection for the Father and a desire to see his will realized in our lives and in our world:

For those who are being led by the Spirit of God, these are the sons of God. For you did not receive a spirit of slavery, for fear again; but you received a Spirit of sonship in which we cry Abba, Father! The Spirit himself bears witness to our spirit that we are children of God. If children, then heirs as well: heirs of God and coheirs of Christ, if indeed we are "co-suffering" so that we will also be "co-glorified."

ROMANS 8:14-17; see GALATIANS 4:4-6

As the *Catechism* teaches us, prayer is "wholly directed to the Father." All the canons of the Mass are thus directed, as are nearly all the prayers of the liturgy that end "through Jesus Christ Our Lord, who lives and reigns with *you* and the Holy Spirit, one God forever and ever." It is for this reason that Jesus teaches us to pray by first turning our heart to the Father, asking him in three different ways to realize his perfect plan on earth and bring it to perfection. We ask that, in a definitive way, God will have his Word return to him from this earth, from our hearts and from all human hearts.

Prayer:

Father, glorify your name! (Jn 12:28). Let the entire world know your love and your faithfulness to your promises. Let your reign take possession of all the world; let evil cease and holiness enter once and for all; let the reality and majesty of your Son be manifest to all. May your plan, your will, be accomplished now and ultimately at the end of history here on earth. We pray, beloved Father, for the vision of your face!

As we live here we pray for all that we need: bread for our bodies and bread for our spirits, as your Wisdom become flesh now gives us the Bread that is his flesh for the life of the world. Forgive us our sins, as we, imitating you, forgive those who have sinned against us. We know, Father, that nothing is closer to your heart than that we forgive each other. We know that you will forgive us from your heart if we will let your word of forgiveness come from our heart and free those who have offended us. As Jesus told his disciples in Gethsemane, we pray to be protected from the final test and to be kept safe from the attacks of the evil one.

Father, let this word, which has come from you onto the soil of your Son's heart, now return from our hearts as well. For yours are the kingdom, and the power, and the glory now and forever. Amen.

✻
Wednesday of the First Week
Jonah 3:1-10; Luke 11:29-32

In the Jewish tradition Jonah is the model preacher of repentance. He may have been a reluctant prophet—he first went in exactly the opposite direction from the one indicated to him by God—but his word to the Ninevites, when they obeyed it, saved their city. It is to this tradition that Jesus is alluding when he invokes the example of Jonah in today's gospel text.

What exactly does the Bible mean by the word "repentance"? The Hebrew word we translate "repent" is *shub*, which means literally "to return," "to retrace one's steps." Another expression is "to seek the Lord." The basic notion is that of turning away from a life of darkness and sin and returning to God. The Greek translation of the Old Testament often used the term *metanoia*, which put the accent on the interior "change of mind" that lies at the root of a change of conduct, without which there is no genuine conversion or repentance.

Part of Jonah's message was that the Ninevites had "forty days" in which to repent. The Church gives us this word about repentance early in our own forty-day period.

A close look at today's texts will help us understand and

enter into this invitation to repentance. Note first that the Lord was so intent on saving Nineveh from the consequences of its sin that, after Jonah's initial disobedience, he spoke to him a "second time." Jonah's word to the Ninevites was that their city would be destroyed in forty days. The reaction to this word was that the people in the city "believed God." Because their hearts were open, they heard and understood that the destruction coming upon their city was the result of their sins. They regretted their sin; they turned from self-indulgence to fasting and so began their return to God.

The Holy Spirit will surely call us to repentance during our own "forty days." It may come through the word of a Jonah in our life, or it may come from an interior action of the Holy Spirit. It is because of his love for us that God points out our sin; he wants us to be free of sin and to come to a greater intimacy with him. Somehow we know this, and when the awareness of sin is brought home to us, there is an experience of joy and release—despite the anger, embarrassment, and resentment we may feel. Truth enters our heart and sets us free. This is an experience of the love of God, and it produces a heartfelt regret and a desire for reconciliation. Like the Ninevites, we "believe God," we desire to be with God, and so we return to him.

There is more, however. We have, in the Church and in our hearts, someone "greater than Jonah," someone who can not only point out our sin to us but give us the power to take authority over that part of our lives and bring it into conformity with God's will. Jesus not only calls us to return; he is the Way by which we return. This is Good News, the gospel that Jesus proclaims to us. In the power of his cross we can really die to sin and live to God. Repentance, therefore, is an interior releasing of our sin and sin patterns to the power of the cross of Christ, the act of love in which he died and rose, so that we can experience new life.

⚜

Thursday of the First Week
Esther 12:14-16, 23-25; Matthew 7:7-12

Yesterday we saw the power of repentance; today the Word of God instructs us on the efficacy of intercession. In the first reading we learn that the secret of intercessory prayer is an honesty and purity of heart before God. In the gospel we hear Our Lord urge us to ask, seek, and knock urgently, counting on the mercy of God.

There is a mystery about intercession. Even if we do not pray very much, when we are in need our instinct is to turn to God and cry out to him. When things are going well and we have the leisure to reflect on the reality of the prayer of intercession and petition, we wonder why there is such a deep instinct in the human heart to pray: surely we are not going to force God to change his mind. But when are we closer to the truth? Is it when we call out to God and somehow hope for a change and even experience his action in our lives, or when we think that asking God for things is in bad taste and we ought only to accept whatever comes?

Since the answer to this question lies in the heart of God, our best approach is to listen to the Word of God and then reflect on what we have learned.

First of all, the psalms, which are a school of prayer, are filled with words of intimacy and petition. For instance, in

42

Psalm 31:15-17 we read: "I trust you, Lord; I say you are my God. My life is in your hands.... Let your face shine on your servant, and save me in your love." And, in Psalm 44:23-26, "Awake! Why are you asleep, O Lord? Rise up! Do not reject us forever. Why do you hide your face, forgetting our misery and suffering?... Arise and come to our aid; for the love you have for us, deliver us."

In addition to the words of the psalms, we have the prayers of Moses and the prophets, and we have the prayer of Jesus himself in Gethsemane. We also have many words of encouragement on the part of Jesus. He even goes so far as to give us the example of the unjust judge who is worn out by the persistent widow, and of the man who finally gets out of bed because his friend keeps knocking on the door (Lk 18:1-8; 11:5-8). And last of all, we have his own instruction: "When you pray say, 'Father, hallowed be your name, your kingdom come. Give us each day our daily bread, and forgive us our sins as we forgive everyone in debt to us'" (Lk 11:1-4).

Clearly, then, we are told in the Scriptures to ask God for things, confident that the Father will never refuse to hear us—and confident too that he will give us what is best. God wants to have a dialogue with us and to be intimate with us. This is a mystery of love and freedom. In thus asking for things of God, we are not to treat him as a benevolent stranger but as a Father. We are not thus "forcing" God; we are interacting with his freedom, which surrounds our own and protects it. God's freedom is beyond our understanding, but this much is clear: he can yield to our requests, even stir us up to ask, without compromising his freedom.

God wants us to pray, to ask, and to intercede, first, so that we will grow in intimacy with him and, second, so that he can accede to our requests. Because intimacy takes time, he sometimes does not answer our prayer right way, so that we will continue to come to him and get to know him.

Thus we see that our basic instinct to pray to God in need is wiser than our rationalizing about God's sovereign will and freedom. This is precisely because, in his sovereign freedom, he wills to be asked and to answer our prayers. He delights in interacting with us. We do not force him; he wants to do what we ask, because he wishes more than anything else to be in a relationship of love and trust with us.

In this spirit, now pray the Our Father and specify what "bread" you want for yourself and for others.

Friday of the First Week

Ezekiel 18:21-28; Matthew 5:20-26

Once again the twofold theme of interiority and community is sounded in the readings the Church gives us. The text from Ezekiel puts before us the awesome mystery of our freedom and its consequences. The principle is laid down: "If the wicked man turns from all the sins he has done and does what is right and just, he shall surely live, he shall not die.... If the just man turns from his justice and does evil, all the abominations done by the wicked, all the just deeds he has done will not be remembered because of the treachery he has done and because of the sin he has committed; because of these things he shall die" (Ez 18:21-24).

To the people's objection that God's way of acting is not "fair," Ezekiel responds that it is Israel's way that is not fair.

Human beings can change: one can change from the way of death to the way of life, and another can do the opposite. This is the power of our freedom.

Often when we think of freedom we think of choice—this or that. But the spiritual root of our freedom lies at the very center of who we are as human beings. Freedom, correctly understood, is the human person's capacity to determine who he or she is. By freedom we "make" ourselves. From deep within our spirit comes the power to move by our actions toward what is good or to move toward what is evil. Our actions determine who we are. The text from Ezekiel in today's liturgy does but place dramatically in front of us the truth that our actions, first interior and then exterior, make us the kind of persons we are.

The words of Jesus in the gospel for today show us that, while our choices spring from the depths of our own interior, our willing of good or evil is most determinative of who we are when relating to another human being. Jesus tells us that not only murder but any action that denies our brother or sister the right to the esteem and respect in which there is a human fullness of life perverts our relationship with them. This wounds and deprives them, as well as ourselves, of the life to which we are all called. Jesus speaks of anger as meriting "the judgment." He further states that external manifestations of that anger—calling someone "*raqa*," that is, contemptible or "fool"—deserve public and eternal punishment.

And then Jesus uncovers for us a mystery that takes our breath away: God is not interested in our liturgical service unless we are reconciled with our brother and sister. "If you bring your gift to the altar, and then remember that your brother has something against you, leave your gift where it is at the altar, go first and be reconciled with your brother, and then come and offer your gift" (Mt 5:23-24).

Prayer:

Lord, you have placed me in front of my freedom and have helped me to see that I am responsible for what I make myself to be. Yet I am not left to my own resources; your Holy Spirit wants to be the power and the deep source of my freedom. At this moment I freely leave myself here before you, and in my heart I seek reconciliation with all those in my family, at work, and anywhere else who have something against me— even if this be that I have not, up till now, forgiven them. I will go to these people, and as much as I can, I will make this reconciliation real and objective between us.

⚜

Saturday of the First Week
Deuteronomy 26:16-19; Matthew 5:43-48

The readings today bring us to much the same place as those of yesterday, and we see in the pedagogy of the Church a deepening of the call of God in our lives. In the first reading we are promised that, if we obey the voice of God, we will be his covenant people and all the world will recognize how blessed we are to be thus called by God. Jesus, in the gospel, takes this another step and holds out before us an even higher vocation: we are to be not only the people through whom God makes himself known to the world but actually imitators of God by our love for everyone.

In the Book of Deuteronomy we hear Moses preaching to the people:

Today you are committing yourself to Yhwh: he is to be your God, and you will walk in his ways and keep his statutes, commandments, and decrees, and obey his voice. And Yhwh commits himself to you this day: you are to be a people especially his own as he told you, keeping all his commands. He will place you up high, praised and renowned, and glorious, above all the nations he has made, and you will be dedicated to Yhwh your God, as he told you.

DEUTERONOMY 26:17-19

God wants to exalt his people and care for them; we are his people if we do what he commands us.

Love and respect for the Word of God comes from a heart that has been broken and freed of self-preoccupation and fear. Listen to this description of the heart of Jesus, the only just man, who was totally faithful to the covenant: "Thus says Yhwh: 'Heaven is my throne and the earth is my footstool; what is the house which you would build for me, and what is the place of my rest? All these things my hand has made, and so all these things are mine,' says Yhwh. But this is the man to whom I will look, he that is humble and contrite in spirit, and trembles at my word" (Is 66:1-2, RSV).

The word to us, a constant refrain in the message of Jesus, is that we are to love everyone. No longer can we love only those with whom we are close and are bound in such a way that we feel "safe" with them. Jesus tells us once again in the gospel today: "Love your enemies and pray for those who persecute you."

Jesus goes on to tell us that in loving everyone rather than looking first to see whether we consider them worthy of our love, we are imitating God and we are his children. We are to be "perfect" as the Father is perfect—that is, we must share in the divine law of love. Like the Father who "makes his sun rise on the bad and the good," we are to love, with an intense personal care, each person we meet. The phrase that best sums this up is found in the Letter to the Ephesians (5:1-2): "Be, then, imitators of God, as beloved children, and walk in love just as Christ loved us, and gave himself over for us, an offering and sacrifice to God as a fragrant odor."

Prayer:

Lord, we are proud to be your people, called by you in sheer mercy and not for any merit of our own. May we always be a people you are proud of. May people see our good works and praise you, our Father in heaven. Amen.

CHAPTER THREE

The Second Week of Lent
Our Call in Christ

The first Sunday of Lent brought us into contact with the two
focal points of our journey up to this point. The first is the fact
of sin and the destruction of sin through the redeeming death
of Our Lord Jesus Christ. The second is the reality of temptation we now face in the power of Jesus' triumph over Satan in
the desert, his triumph over Satan in all of his life, and finally
his triumph over Satan at the cross.

Most of the daily readings spoke of our need for genuine
interiority and authentic relatedness in Christ. We are shown
Christ in the poor and needy and are also brought to face the
scandal of division and the need for reconciliation in the Body
of Christ.

The second Sunday in the initial period of preparation
draws us—catechumens, candidates, and full members of the
Church—toward the glorious goal of our call in Christ Jesus.
The daily readings initiate us more deeply into the second of
the themes of Lent, sin and forgiveness, and the relationship
of this to the mystery of Christ's death and resurrection.

Sunday of the Second Week

Genesis 12:1-4; 2 Timothy 1:8-10; Matthew 17:1-9

God calls us to glory. He calls us to leave our familiar boredom and fear and set out for a land he will show us, a land whose promise is beyond our timid desires and whose reality answers the desires we are almost afraid to mention. Deep within each of us is the desire for a love that is without any shadow of deceit. We want to be in union with Someone who loves us in this way—Someone who has the power to bring us to an unending share in his life, a Person who will help us and forgive us and give us a life, in both body and spirit, that will last forever. The wonder is that we are called to such a reality. Those who hear this call and treasure it, who believe in the One who calls us and respond to him in trust, make the journey to that land.

Abraham, our father in faith, heard such a call, and in response "he set out not knowing where he was to go" (Heb 11:8, RSV). Here is a man undistinguished by anything. All we know of him before his call is that he was insignificant—one of three sons of a certain Terah, and married to a woman who had borne him no children. Then, out of nowhere, came the call of the Lord: "Go out from your land, and your clan, and your father's house to a land that I will show you. I will make of you a great nation [a childless man!], and I will bless you. I will make your name great [an insignificant nomad!].... And Abram went as Yhwh told him" (Gn 12:1-4).

It is a testament to Abraham's greatness that, despite lapses, he continued to believe and to obey and thus became the

father of a race that imitated him and became our ancestors
We are the people who now possess, though as yet only in
faith, the glorious land for which he and Israel became
nomads of faith. Here is how the Letter to the Hebrews
describes them:

> In faith, all these died, not having obtained the promises,
> but they saw them from afar and hailed them and pro-
> fessed that they were strangers and sojourners on the
> earth. They, saying such things, made evident that they
> were looking for a homeland; and if they had in mind
> that from which they came out, they would have had
> occasion to return. But now they aspire to one that is bet-
> ter, that is, heavenly. For this reason, God is not ashamed
> of them, to be called their God; he prepared a city for
> them.... And all of these were attested to through faith,
> yet they did not obtain the promise; God foreseeing
> something better concerning us, so that not without us
> would they be made perfect.
>
> HEBREWS 11:13-16, 39-40

The Second Letter to Timothy reminds us that we, like
Abraham, are called. Yet while we now possess in faith what
Abraham could only salute from afar, we must still face hard-
ship responding to our "holy calling, not according to our
own works but according to his plan and the grace he conferred on us in Christ Jesus before the ages." This calling is
now available and efficacious because Our Lord Jesus Christ
has appeared, "who abolished death and brought life and
immortality to light through the gospel" (2 Tm 1:8-10, RSV).
In sounding the theme of life and immortality, we are

given a glimpse of the land that the Lord will show us. The Transfiguration of Jesus, presented to us in the gospel, shows us clearly not only Jesus' glory but the glory to which we ourselves are called. In some mysterious anticipation of the glory that would be his after the Resurrection, Jesus, having just predicted his passion a few days previously, was transfigured before three of his disciples.

The Preface of the Mass today speaks of Jesus' desire to teach his disciples, through the Law and the prophets (Moses and Elijah), that "the promised Christ had first to suffer and so come to the glory of his resurrection." When the Feast of the Transfiguration is celebrated on August 6, the Preface accents the other aspect of this mystery: "His glory shone from a body like our own, to show that the Church which is the Body of Christ would one day share his glory."

This is the goal of our pilgrimage: to be transformed, body and soul, by the divine Trinitarian life and to live overjoyed by his love forever. Encourage one another with this thought of the goal God has in his heart for us, and help each other to obey his call as did Abraham, our father in faith.

❧

Monday of the Second Week
Daniel 9:4-10; Luke 6:36-38

Today we are taught two of the key secrets to peace of heart: honest acknowledgment of sin and forgiveness of others. Our hearts are so overburdened sometimes that we become sick, and the reason is often that we guard guile in our hearts.

Psalm 32 teaches us the way to freedom and healing. The

psalm begins with two "beatitudes": "Blessed is that one whose fault is taken away, whose sin is covered. Blessed is the man to whom the Lord imputes no guilt, and in whose spirit there is no guile." We might be tempted to think that the last part of the second beatitude refers to a moral quality, a certain self-acquired honesty, but in reality it refers to the effect of having our sins forgiven by God. We are liars, we are full of guile, because we are covering over our sin rather than acknowledging it before God and receiving his forgiveness.

Listen to the story the psalmist tells us: "When I kept silence my bones wasted away, with moaning all day long. Day and night your hand was heavy on me.... Then I acknowledged my sin to you; I did not cover my guilt. I said: 'I confess my rebellion to the Lord.' And you lifted off the guilt of my sin" (Ps 32:3-5). As a free man, no longer obliged to cover over the depths of his heart, the psalmist goes on to encourage others, urging them not to be senseless, unable to be curbed except by bit and bridle. And he concludes: "Rejoice in the Lord and dance, all you just ones; sing, all you of upright heart!"

In light of this deep spiritual principle we can understand the honesty and purity of heart expressed in Daniel's prayer: "We have sinned, doing what is wrong and wicked.... We have not obeyed your servants the prophets.... O Lord, justice is on your side; on our side shame covers our face.... But yours, O Lord, are compassion and forgiveness" (Dn 9:5-7, 9). This is the truth, and the truth sets us free. We are often afraid of acknowledging our real situation to God, the only one who can help us, and yet this is the way to peace. Someone once asked St. Thérèse of Lisieux what she would do if she had just committed a very great sin. She answered, "I would run straight to God. I know that he can and will help me."

In the gospel we see the other side of the lack of guile born of honest acknowledgment of sin: we forgive others. "Don't judge, and you will not be judged. Don't condemn, and you will not be condemned. Forgive and you will be forgiven.... For the measure you give to others will in turn be measured out to you."

St. Paul echoes this teaching of Jesus when he tells us to bear with one another, to forgive one another if there is any grievance between us: "As the Lord has forgiven you, so you must do likewise" (Col 3:13). Forgiveness does not mean trying to construe someone's sin against us as not really wrong. It does mean learning the awesome power of the forgiveness set loose by Jesus' act of love on the cross. There, fully aware that he was being sinned against, he prayed for forgiveness for those who crucified him.

Prayer:

Thank you, Lord, for this guidance to peace—peace in our hearts and peace in our midst. Each of us, personally and at this moment, confesses our sins against you and against others. Confident of your mercy and love, we receive your forgiveness and hasten to share it with our sisters and brothers. Amen.

⚜

Tuesday of the Second Week
Isaiah 1:10, 16-20; Matthew 23:1-12

We can get some idea of the importance of repentance for sin in the Christian life by considering the number of times during Lent that the Church invokes biblical passages that call us to acknowledge our sin and turn from it. The Holy Spirit uses the Word of God to bring us to an experiential knowledge of having our sin pointed out by God and of the freedom he encourages us to receive. When the reality of our sin is first brought home to us two things happen: there is shock at the truth of our sin, discomfort, and some fear; but there is also relief, for the truth has begun to set us free. The words of Isaiah have that result in our hearts if we listen.

Though the text from Isaiah is edited in our liturgical form (verses 11-15 about empty ceremonial worship are omitted), the opening lines are there and addressed to us. We are told to "hear the word of the Lord" and "listen to the teaching of our God." But we are also addressed as "princes of Sodom" and "people of Gomorrah." Are we really that bad? The answer is yes, but the irony is that only those who have let the Holy Spirit purify their hearts and bring them into a relationship of love and trust with the Father are capable of appreciating this. For most of us, sin itself has clouded our minds, and the fascination of life's daily trifles keeps us from a clear vision of reality.

We have to look to the saints to find that robust honesty and trust in God that this text calls us to. We read that the saints wept over their sins, not only those of their past life but also the reticences and infidelities of every day. We may wonder if this is not just some morbid preoccupation with sin. But when we read their works and sense their joy—or even better, when we meet someone who is being transformed by the love of Christ—we see that holiness and morbidity are simply incompatible.

These people are grateful for the mercy and love God has shown to them. It is love that makes them weep for the ways they still resist Jesus, just as it is clarity that allows them to see their past. Listen, for instance, to St. Teresa of Avila commenting on her past life: "May His Majesty be pleased to pardon me, for I have been the cause of many evils, but not with the intention of doing all the harm that was afterward the outcome of my deeds."[1]

The next part of the Isaiah text instructs us on how to practice justice: "Learn to do good; seek justice, correct oppression; defend the fatherless, plead for the widow" (Is 1:17, RSV). Then come the freedom and sense of trust that always accompany God's action in convincing us of our sin: "Come now, let us reason together, says the Lord: though your sins are like scarlet, they shall be as white as snow; though they are red like crimson, they shall become like wool" (Is 1:18, RSV).

In our Lord's words from Matthew's Gospel we can sense the same rhythm of conviction and encouragement. Jesus first points out the sins of the scribes and Pharisees, most especially their lack of compassion for those who are struggling to keep God's law and their love of human recognition and honor. He then addresses the Christians, and Matthew makes sure that we realize that these words are addressed to us, especially to leaders in the Christian community. He tells us not to wish to be called "Rabbi," which means "honored teacher," since we have only one honored teacher, Jesus Christ. Also, we should call no one on earth our father, since we have only one Father in heaven.

This means that no human being ("on earth") is to be considered the ultimate source of life, especially spiritual life, and no one should want to be so considered. We must first recognize that God the Father is he "from whom every family takes its name in heaven and on earth" (Eph 3:15). Then, in humility, it is not amiss to give the title to someone who deserves it, as Paul once remarked: "For though you have countless guides in Christ, you do not have many fathers. For I became your father in Christ Jesus through the gospel" (1 Cor 4:15, RSV). Finally, as in the text from Isaiah, comes the word of encouragement and freedom: "Whoever exalts himself will be humbled, and whoever humbles himself will be exalted" (Mt 23:12, RSV).

⚜

Wednesday of the Second Week
Jeremiah 18:18-20; Matthew 20:17-28

Today the shadow of the cross is visible. In the first reading we see something of the soul of Jesus in the prayer of Jeremiah. In the gospel we are told of the mystery of the cross, and our lack of understanding is challenged.

Even more than his words, Jeremiah's life was a prophecy. He embraced the will and Word of God even when it led him into suffering. So powerful was his life that when a later author composed what we call the second part of Isaiah and included there the description of the one to come who would reconcile God's people by his suffering, the model he alluded to was Jeremiah. The prayer of this prophet has become the Word of God:

"Come, let us make plots against Jeremiah ... Come, let us smite him with the tongue, and let us not heed any of his words...." Give heed to me, O Lord, and hearken to my plea. Is evil a recompense for good? Yet they have dug a pit for my life. Remember how I stood before you to speak good for them, to turn away your wrath from them.

For the first time in Lent we encounter one of those Old Testament texts that may be called a "sacrament" of the soul of Jesus. Jeremiah was one of those suffering just men whose life and prayer constituted an anticipated share in the fullness of grace in Jesus Christ which we all receive. The human pain of rejection and treachery was one of the greatest sufferings Jesus had to endure. Yet by his fidelity to the covenant (he being the only one who perfectly kept the covenant) we have been saved. This prayer of Jeremiah will lead us into the sanctuary of the very heart of Jesus and help us to understand why his love led him to suffer for us.

The gospel text introduces us to the manner in which the synoptic Gospels, particularly Matthew and Mark, present Jesus' prediction of his death and resurrection. In both of these Gospels there are three predictions recorded. Each follows a specific threefold rhythm, probably due to the theological editing work of the evangelists. There is first a prediction of Jesus, then a completely inept response on the part of the disciples, and finally teaching by Jesus on the nature of discipleship. The purpose of this rhythm is not primarily to show us how little the disciples understood the meaning of what Jesus was to do for us but to show us how little we still understand and why.

In today's text, the third of the Passion predictions, Jesus speaks of his upcoming betrayal, the torture he will undergo, his death, and his vindication by the Father. Immediately afterward James and John seek the first places in the kingdom, and the rest of the disciples become indignant. Finally, Jesus teaches them about the true meaning of leadership in the community: "Whoever would be great among you must be your servant, and whoever would be first among you must be your slave; even as the Son of Man came not to be served but to serve, and to give his life as a ransom for many" (Mt 20:26-28, RSV).

Prayer:

Lord Jesus, you have shown us your own inner life, your suffering, and your complete willingness to serve us by laying down your life for us. Please take from us our willingness to disregard the dignity and rights of others so that we can have first place. Help us to follow the model you have taught us by your words and deeds. Amen.

Thursday of the Second Week
Jeremiah 17:5-10; Luke 16:19-31

By placing these two texts side by side the Church has enabled us to see them both in a very particular light. We are thus led to see how our lack of trust in God drives us to acquire wealth for ourselves—whether this be in money, esteem, education, pleasure, or social advantage. This ambition blinds us to the true meaning of life and keeps us in bondage to a fear that our wealth cannot assuage.

In the first part of the Jeremiah text we find a contrast between the one who trusts in human resources and the one who trusts in God: "Cursed is the man who trusts in man and makes flesh his arm, whose heart turns away from the Lord. He is like a shrub in the desert, and shall not see any good come.... Blessed is the man who trusts in the Lord, whose confidence is the Lord. He is like a tree planted by water, that sends out its roots by the stream." Then, in an allusion to the deep wellsprings of the choice for one way of living or the other, Jeremiah goes on: "The heart is deceitful above all things, and desperately corrupt; who can understand it? 'I the Lord search the mind and try the heart, to give to every man according to his ways, according to the fruit of his doings'" (Jer 17:5-10, RSV).

The parable that Jesus tells us is meant to bring healing for the deceit in our hearts. He tells us of a rich man who "feasted sumptuously every day" while a poor man named Lazarus (his name means "God is my help") sat at the door of the mansion. Lazarus, "covered with sores,... would have been happy to eat the crumbs that fell from the rich man's table." Lazarus died and was borne to Abraham's bosom; the rich man died and was buried. This frightening contrast illustrates what may be called "the law of reversal." "Blessed are you poor, the kingdom of God is yours.... Woe to you rich, you have received your consolation" (Lk 6:20, 24).

The rich man called out to Abraham, asking that Lazarus dip his finger in water and come to cool his tongue. Abraham replied first by enunciating the principle of reversal: "Son, remember that you in your lifetime received your good things, and Lazarus in like manner evil things; but now he is comforted here, and you are in anguish" (Lk 16:25, RSV). He then added that there was such a chasm between them that Lazarus could never cross.

Next, the tormented rich man began to plead for his brothers. He asked Abraham to send Lazarus to warn them. Abraham replied that they had all the teaching they needed, Moses and the prophets. The rich man insisted, "No, father Abraham, but if someone goes to them from the dead, then they will repent." Abraham replied, "If they do not hear Moses and the prophets, neither will they be convinced if someone should rise from the dead."

The law of reversal means simply that things are not what they appear to be. The rich and powerful, who ignore the suffering of their brothers and sisters, are really the ones whose lives are a failure: life is not measured by this world's power. The poor man, on the other hand, represents the person, man or woman, who delights in depending upon God and cultivates a way of life that keeps this experience alive in some solidarity with the Lazaruses of this world. Such a person is "like a tree planted by water," bearing the fruit of compassion. While people may exclaim, "Why this waste?" when they see the manner of such a person's life, there is hidden within it the seed of glory.

The answer, then, is to beg God for the grace to trust him and depend upon him, and in the power of that grace to shed those things that can insulate us from this secret of freedom and joy. We will thus acquire a heart that knows where true wealth really lies.

✣

Friday of the Second Week
Genesis 37:3-4, 12-13, 17-28; Matthew 21:33-46

Today we are brought once again into contact with the mystery of the Lord's passion and death. The theme is the rejection of the beloved son. In the first reading we hear of Joseph, the beloved of Jacob, first assaulted and then sold into slavery by his own brothers. In the gospel text Jesus tells his own countrymen a parable concerning the rejection and murder of the only son of the vineyard owner.

There is a mystery hidden here. Why is it that our rejection of Christ has brought about our acceptance by the Father? The depths of mercy contained in this mystery can take our breath away. It is perhaps for this reason that we are given glimpses of this radiant white light only in a refracted form. We see it in foreshadowings such as the Joseph story, in parables such as the one today, in cryptic phrases such as Our Lord's predictions of his passion ("[He will] be rejected by the elders, the chief priests, and scribes" [Lk 9:22, RSV]), and in oblique phrases in the rest of the New Testament.

The story of Joseph is well-known. The firstborn son of Rachel, whom Jacob loved more than Leah; the object of his father's special attention, symbolized by the beautiful tunic he conferred on him—Joseph was hated by his brothers. The text today tells us of their treachery. They first threw Joseph into a dry cistern to die in the desert heat, and then they took him out and sold him as a slave to a caravan bound for Egypt. There Joseph rose to prominence but was falsely accused, imprisoned, then finally released and installed over the whole land of Egypt.

During a severe famine Joseph's brothers came to this ruler of Egypt for aid. On their second visit he made as if to imprison his full brother Benjamin, and then he could bear it no longer. As his brothers pleaded for the life of Benjamin, Joseph began to weep. He cleared the audience hall, revealed himself to his brothers, and then enunciated the meaning of his rejection: "And now do not be distressed, or angry with yourselves, because you sold me here; for God sent me before you to preserve life." Still later, after Jacob's death, his brothers came to him, afraid that now Joseph would take his revenge. Once again we hear pronounced the law of our redemption: "As for you, you meant evil against me; but God meant it for good, to bring it about that many people should be kept alive, as they are today" (see Gn 45:5; 50:20).

The chief priests and Pharisees know that Jesus' parable is about themselves (see Mt 21:45). Drawing on conditions in Galilee of the time, with rich absentee landowners and sullen tenant farmers, Jesus tells a story about the vineyard, already declared by Isaiah to be Israel (see Is 5:1-7). The tenant farmers abuse the agents sent to collect the owner's share of the produce, and finally, when the owner sends what must be his only son, they kill him, expecting to be able to take over the vineyard now that the heir is dead.

Jesus' audience predicts what will come of such murderers: The owner will come, and "he will put those wretches to a wretched death, and let out the vineyard to other tenants who will give him the fruits in their seasons." Jesus goes on to draw out clearly the mystery of rejection, using this time Psalm 118:22-23: "Have you never read in the scriptures: 'The very stone which the builders rejected has become the head of the corner; this was the Lord's doing, and it is marvelous in our eyes'?"

How can we describe the mystery of God's willingness to bring life out of the death we cause? "For our sake [God] made [Christ] to be sin who knew no sin, so that in him we might become the righteousness of God" (2 Cor 5:21, RSV); and again: "For you know the grace of our Lord Jesus Christ, that though he was rich, yet for your sake he became poor, so that by his poverty you might become rich" (2 Cor 8:9, RSV). Only the Holy Spirit can lead us into the unfathomable depths of God's reckless love for us, the Creator of the universe willing to be rejected in order to transform our depravity into a grateful return of love.

❦

Saturday of the Second Week
Micah 7:14-15, 18-20; Luke 15:1-3, 11-32

Friday's theme is taken up again today, this time accenting the Father's forgiveness and its source, his loyal love for us. The beautiful text of Micah praises God as unique, declaring, "What god is like you? You forgive guilt; you pass over sin for the remnant of your inheritance. You do not prolong your anger forever; no, your delight is in love and pardon" (Mi 7:18). Today's gospel text is one of the most important in the New Testament, since in this parable of the Prodigal Son (really that of the Generous Father), Jesus reveals his own knowledge of the Father to us.

Everyone knows the story: "A man had two sons." The younger one (who had a right to one-third of the property) demanded his share of the estate, thus considering his father as good as dead. The father, in a gesture that defied cultural norms, gave the younger son his share of the estate. This the son transformed into liquid assets and took with him to a "far off country." There he spent all his inheritance on loose living. One of the local gentry employed him, a Jew, to feed the pigs. When he found himself yearning to eat the pigs' food, he "came to himself," realizing that his father's day laborers were better off than he. He resolved, "I will get up and go to my father, and I will say to him, 'Father, I have sinned against heaven and before you; I am no longer worthy to be called your son; treat me as one of your day laborers.' And he got up and went back to his father."

In the next section of the parable Jesus reveals the heart of the Father:

> But while he was yet at a distance, his father saw him and was filled with compassion, and ran and embraced him and kissed him. And the son said to him, "Father, I have sinned against heaven and before you; I am no longer worthy to be called your son." [He never finishes his prepared speech.] But the father said to his servants, "Quickly, bring the best robe, and put it on him; and put a ring on his hand, and sandals on his feet; and bring the fatted calf and kill it, and let us eat and make merry; for this my son was dead, and is alive again; he was lost, and is found." And they began to make merry.

The father not only had compassion, running out to meet his son and embracing him; he not only restored the boy to his former dignity, giving him a robe, a ring, and sandals; but he was so full of joy that he declared a feast. The father had never renounced the truth of his relationship to the son, and he acted on it. This is mercy, a movement of love based on the truth and the profound justice contained in the relationship.

Mercy looks to the person; pity looks to the need. Our Father has mercy and never parts from it: he is loyal to the relationship he has established with us in Christ. His heart beats faster when he sees us returning to him. As Pope John Paul II expresses it: "This prodigal son is man, every human being.... Like the father in the parable, God looks out for the return of his child, embraces him when he arrives, and orders the banquet of the new meeting with which the reconciliation is celebrated" (*Reconciliation and Penance,* N.5).

The older son, who never left home but who had not had such a banquet in his honor, often elicits from us sympathy and a sense of identification. Perhaps we, too, serve the Father and "never once disobey," but more to secure our own safety than out of love for the Father. We would rather be "safe," based on our performance, than free, based on the Father's love. Such a freedom frightens us. May this parable move us into that realm of freedom. Let us obey and trust in a movement of love based on the truth of who the Father is and of his relationship to us.

CHAPTER FOUR

The Third Week of Lent
The Thirst for Christ

The third Sunday of Lent marks a significant point in the journey toward Easter. The Church, accompanying the catechumens, begins to open up for them the greatness of the gift to come. At the same time we who are already believers are enabled to deepen our own faith appreciation of Christ, "in whom are hid all the treasures of wisdom and knowledge" (Col 2:3, RSV), and to have our hearts purified by a desire for him. The next three Sundays show us the Paschal Mystery, the mystery of the death and resurrection of Christ, using the symbols of water, light, and life.

These same Sundays are characterized by three "scrutinies," or purifications from evil, which, while they are special prayers for those preparing for baptism, are meant to help us all. The *Rite of Christian Initiation of Adults* speaks of the scrutinies in these terms: "The scrutinies are meant to uncover, then heal, all that is weak, defective, or sinful in the hearts of the elect; to bring out, then strengthen, all that is upright, strong, and good. In the rite of exorcism ... the elect, who have already learned from the Church—as their mother—the mystery of deliverance from sin by Christ, are freed from the effects of sin and from the influence of the devil."[1] Though we are now sealed by baptism, we too need to have the Holy Spirit uncover and heal in our own lives "all that is weak, defective, or sinful" and to "strengthen all that is upright, strong, and good." We, too, need to be set free from "the effects of sin and... the influence of the devil."

The actual prayer recited by the Church on the occasion of the scrutiny this Sunday is one that we can repeat for the catechumens and for ourselves several times during the week. To that purpose it is here rewritten in the first person:

> Lord Jesus, you are the fountain for which we thirst, you are the Master whom we seek. In your presence we dare not claim to be without sin, for you alone are the Holy One of God. We open our hearts to you in faith; we confess our faults and lay bare our hidden wounds. In your love free us from our infirmities, heal our sickness, quench our thirst, and give us peace. In the power of your name, which we call upon in faith, stand by us now and heal us. Rule over that spirit of evil, which was conquered by your rising from the dead. Show us the way of salvation in the Holy Spirit, so that we may come to worship the Father in truth, for you live and reign forever and ever. Amen."[2]

One of the realities of our spirit uncovered by the Word of God today is precisely our thirst for God and our desire to know him with certitude, free from the illusions and shadows cast by our sins. It is this reality that Jesus addresses when he promises the Samaritan woman: "If anyone drinks the water I will give them, they will not thirst for ever; rather the water that I will give them will become in them a fountain of bubbling water for eternal life" (Jn 4:14).

Jesus is promising the Holy Spirit. The woman asks for this water and is told to get her husband. Jesus turns her evasive answer into an "uncovering" of her sin: "The man you have now is not your husband." When she asks about the meaning of worship Jesus says, "True worshipers will worship the Father in Spirit and in truth; indeed, the Father seeks such people to worship him." We are to worship the Father in the power of the Holy Spirit, the living water, and in the revelation of the Father brought by Christ, who is the Truth ("I am the Way, the Truth, and the Life" [Jn 14:6, RSV]).

Jesus is promising to assuage our thirst, to bring us, even now, to a life-changing vision of the Father's face, looking on us with love and mercy. There we are set free from our illusions and fears and come to a confidence in the Father that no one can take from us. Let us pray to him every day this week and ask: "Free us from our infirmities, heal our sickness, quench our thirst, and give us peace. Amen."

Monday of the Third Week
2 Kings 5:1-15; Luke 4:24-30

The theme of water is continued today. The first reading gives us Naaman as an example of someone who was ultimately willing to believe that the apparently ordinary waters of the Jordan River could actually bring him healing through the power of the Word of God. In the gospel Jesus uses Naaman as an example of God's care for those who apparently do not belong to his people. In the obvious allusion to Baptism, we are challenged to look at the mystery of sacramentality in ordinary things. In Jesus' application we are brought to compare the narrowness of our view of who is "worthy" with the breadth and mercy of God's view of things. Let us now concentrate on the first of these lessons and learn something about faith.

Naaman, a leper and general of the armies of the king of Aram, directed by the advice of a Hebrew slave girl and armed with a letter from his king, goes to the king of Israel seeking healing. The king can only see in the request some pretext for a conflict stirred up by Aram, but Elisha hears of it and tells the Israelite king to send Naaman to him: "Let him come to me and learn that there is a prophet in Israel"(2 Kgs 5:8). The prophet can see God's intention where the king can see only politics.

Naaman goes to Elisha expecting a personal meeting and a cure through some dramatic gesture. Elisha, however, merely sends word to him to go and wash in the Jordan seven times. Naaman turns away in anger and disgust. The general can see only an ordinary bath where the prophet can see the power of God. Finally, persuaded by his servants, Naaman goes to the waters of the Jordan and bathes: "So he went down and dipped himself seven times in the Jordan, according to the word of the man of God; and his flesh was restored like the flesh of a little child, and he was clean" (2 Kgs 5:14, RSV).

Faith is a way of knowing. It is a God-given share in his own light, an ability to know God and all other things just as God knows them. St. Thomas Aquinas calls faith "a certain imprint of the divine knowledge." Faith enables us to see "what is really going on" in the world in which we live. It is a certain flair for reality.

Imagine, for instance, that you and a friend are at a concert.

The orchestra is playing the works of Beethoven or Mozart, and the hall is permeated by these beautiful sounds in such a way that you are lifted and filled with delight. When the concert is over, you turn to your friend and say: "Wasn't that wonderful?" only to hear, "I'm bored. Let's get out of here." There was something there to be "gotten," but your friend didn't "get" it. He has no flair for music, no ability to grasp what is there to be appreciated.

In the story from the Book of Kings, the general, and especially the king, cannot appreciate the movement of God, but the prophet can: his faith makes him sensitive to the Word of God being addressed right here and now. He "knows" beyond knowing; he can catch the perfume of God's presence in the air, and he yields to this evidence beyond evidence. Growth in faith is much the same for all of us: we yield to what we "know" is true even though this knowledge is not under our control but is rather mediated to us by the active interior witness of the Holy Spirit.

Faith is a risk, not because what God is telling us might be false but because we cannot control the knowledge. Apply this principle, for instance, to the sacraments. We know that the sacraments are not mere ceremonies but actions of Jesus Christ, who never fails to act in and through the sacraments when they are celebrated in faith (which is also his action in us). When you are at the liturgy, try to catch the "scent" of the presence and action of Christ. Be open to him in his Word, in the assembly around you, and especially in the gift of the Eucharist. Like Naaman, you will discover the healing power of God.

Tuesday of the Third Week
Daniel 3:25, 34-43; Matthew 18:21-35

The readings today return us to the most basic theme of Jesus' teaching regarding our relationships: forgiveness. We are to forgive one another, "as God in Christ forgave you" (Eph 4:32, RSV). In the Book of Daniel we learn how to pray for forgiveness; in the gospel we learn about the one thing the Father expects of us if we are to receive his forgiveness. Daniel's prayer is a model of heartfelt repentance that not only looks at one's personal sins but recognizes that as a people we have sullied God's reputation in this world by the way that we live. In the gospel Jesus teaches us that mutual love and forgiveness are precisely the way he expects us to live in this world. This is our witness, making the salvation he brought about credible to those who see us: "This is how all will know that you are my disciples, if you have love for one another" (Jn 13:35).

In our gospel text, Peter wants to know how many times he should forgive a brother who has sinned against him. He is willing to go as high as seven times. Jesus' answer basically tells Peter to stop counting. Then he tells this story, which, as is often the case with Jesus' parables, is marked by an exuberance of numbers and details. It may help as well to know that in Aramaic, our Lord's native language, the word for "debt" and the word for "sin" are the same.

In this parable, a king decides to collect his debts, and someone is brought in who owes him ten thousand talents. Ten thousand is the highest number the ancients ever used in calculating (after that it became "innumerable"), while a "talent" was the largest monetary unit known. The total tax levy on the entire province of Judea for one year was six hundred talents. Obviously the figure Jesus uses means that the man for some reason owes what he could never repay.

The indebted servant pleads with the king, "Be patient with me, and I will pay you in full," something he could never do. The king forgives his debt. The servant goes out and spots another servant who owes him what would be a laborer's wages for four months. He throttles him, refuses his plea for patience and his promise to repay, and sends him off to prison until his relatives can raise the amount.

The disproportion between the two debts is staggering, and Jesus means to stagger us. The king hears of this, "and in anger his lord delivered him to the jailers, till he should pay all his debt. So also my heavenly Father will do to every one of you, if you do not forgive your brother from your heart" (Mt 18:34-35, RSV).

Only the saints know how great is the debt against us, cancelled by the Father because of the blood of his Son. Overwhelmed by mercy, only they know how to forgive "from the heart." We can learn both these aspects of forgiveness from the Holy Spirit, if we ask. Such a prayer is optimistic; it knows that no sin is unpardonable. Even if some unjust sufferings seem to surpass our capacity to grasp and thus to release (think of the Holocaust, of Hiroshima, of Littleton), still we know that by the grace of God the human spirit can be greater than the injustice and *can* forgive it. There are examples all around us of those who have so forgiven, and they are proofs to us of how great human beings can be.

In our own lives there are often sufferings that have been imposed on us: childhood abuse, spousal abuse, deep rejection. When we bring these to Jesus we must be honest. First, we must acknowledge before him that we have been sinned against. Sometimes this is hard enough. Then we must quietly tell him, "I forgive the person who has committed this injury." Do not worry about your emotions; just say those words, perhaps in prayer with another. That movement of your heart shares in the infinity of God's mercy. Finally, we must also repent for the anger that has been in our own heart. In this way we come to experience even more deeply the freedom of knowing how much we are forgiven, and in some mysterious way we lift a burden from the other person.

⚜

Wednesday of the Third Week
Deuteronomy 4:1, 5-9; Matthew 5:17-19

Jesus is the only man who ever kept the covenant perfectly. In his love for his Father he cherished every indication of the Father's will, and he taught us to do the same. The readings we have today accent one aspect of that fidelity, while the readings for Thursday and Friday of this week accent other aspects.

The first reading today is from the Book of Deuteronomy, the fifth and last book of the Law, or Torah. Deuteronomy is the Greek title for the book, and it means "the second law." It resumes and advances the thinking of the first four books of the Law. Moses is presented as a preacher who personalizes the previous legislation and exhorts Israel to obedience. Two results of this obedience are listed for us: first, "you may live, and go in and take possession of the land"; second, in seeing Israel's way of life the other nations will say, "Surely this great nation is a wise and understanding people." Finally, Moses exhorts the people, "Only take heed, and keep your soul diligently, lest you forget the things which your eyes have seen, and lest they depart from your heart all the days of your life."

Let us now listen to Jesus, the new Moses: "Do not think that I have come to abolish the law or the prophets. I have not come to abolish but to fulfill." And then he urges us, "Whoever does these commandments and teaches them shall be called great in the kingdom of heaven." We are called then to be like Jesus and to fulfill the law. We do this in the power of the Holy Spirit, whom Jesus poured out on Pentecost.

But what does it mean to "fulfill"? Think of this example. We are at a dinner party, but for some reason there is nothing to drink. I get up and say, "I'll find something." People presume I am going to bring water, but then I come back with a tray decked with glasses of a delicious wine. I have not met their expectations; I have *fulfilled* them.

So Jesus, in being faithful to the will of his Father, did not merely meet the prophetic expectations of his people or the expectations of the law, he *fulfilled* them. He went beyond them, cherishing them and bringing them to an unsuspected and glorious consummation. He enables us to do the same. As St. Paul says, "The just requirement of the law is fulfilled in us who walk, not according to the flesh, but according to the Spirit" (Rom 8:4). By the work of the Holy Spirit we can participate in the very inner life of Christ, we can love the Father and call him "Abba," and we can entrust our lives to him. Rather than do his will while still wishing to be doing something else, we can be so changed that we love his will and live out the new covenant with all the enthusiasm of our heart.

Such an ideal is not unrealistic; it is simply the call of the gospel. Listen to the way St. Paul describes this, and let the

75

Spirit witness to you of its possibility in your own life: "Owe no one anything, except to love one another; for he who loves his neighbor has fulfilled the law.... Love does no wrong to a neighbor; therefore love is the fulfillment of the law" (Rom 13:8-10, RSV).

♣
Thursday of the Third Week
Jeremiah 7:23-28; Luke 11:14-23

Just as obedience and trust bring about an enlargement of our heart and a deeper freedom, so disobedience and lack of trust bring about hardness of heart and slavery. That is the lesson of the readings we have today.

It is often instructive to see how the Church uses the respon-sorial psalm after the first reading to accent the truth that links this reading to the gospel. Today we sing in the psalm: "If today you hear the Lord's voice, harden not your hearts" (Ps 95:8).

The verses we have today from chapter seven of the Book of Jeremiah constitute the concluding lines of the record of a speech God commanded Jeremiah to give at the gates of the temple. Jeremiah's description of the people's disobedience is unrelenting: "From the day that your fathers came out of the land of Egypt to this day, I have persistently sent all my servants the prophets to them, day after day; yet they did not listen to me, or incline their ear, but stiffened their neck. They did worse than their fathers" (Jer 7:25-26, RSV).

Such prophetic condemnations are frightening because, as the great Fathers of the Church and the spiritual masters remind us, sin is the punishment for sin. We can go from one depth of sin to another, all the while hardly realizing how dull our spirits have become, until finally perversity seems normal.

We see that same spiritual law at work in the conflict between Jesus and some in the crowd who have just seen him cast out a mute spirit. They charge him with being in collusion with Beelzebul, the prince of demons. Jesus answers the charge of collusion and then warns them: "He who is not with me is against me, and he who does not gather with me scatters" (Lk 11:23, RSV).

Still others in the crowd ask Jesus for a sign. These people want to be forced to believe. The fault of those who look for a sign is pervasive; it is based on a refusal to go out of oneself in faith. And it leads to hardness of heart. The law of faith, on the other hand, is realized in those who yield ever more deeply to the divine realities made known to us by God.

The great truths of reality, as in their own way the scientists can tell us, are not discovered by carefully controlled experiments but by a leap of the spirit, an intuition, a yielding to what is greater than we are. In fact, it is a law that the greater the truth, the more of the human person is involved in its knowing. If you challenge my statement that water begins to expand at four degrees Celsius, I can give you a glass of water and a thermometer and invite you to put the glass in the freezer. You will be compelled despite yourself by the empirical evidence to acknowledge the truth of the statement. If, however, I tell you that the works of Cézanne or Michelangelo are profound interpretations of reality and you challenge me, all I can do is stand you there before them. You will not be "compelled" despite yourself to see what is there. You will have to yield to their witness: more of you must be involved, and you may feel a call to risk in order to enter into their truth.

Suppose, finally, I tell you that Jesus Christ is the eternal Son of God who by his human death and resurrection has reconciled the whole human race to the Father, and as a result, eternal life is being offered to you. You stand there before this truth, but it will take all of you this time to yield to the interior witness of the Holy Spirit and come to know and experience this reality. This is God's invitation at every moment.

Even if you already believe, take a moment now to yield to this witness. Let this law of faith bring you ever more deeply into union with God.

Friday of the Third Week
Hosea 14:2-10; Mark 12:28-34

Purity of heart consists in loving God above all else. Israel learned this from God himself and recited it three times every day in the famous *Shema:* "Hear, O Israel. The Lord is our God, the Lord alone. And you shall love the Lord, your God, with all your heart and all your soul and all your strength" (Dt 6:4-5).

In the first reading today, from the prophet Hosea, God himself is calling upon his people to abandon their fruitless search for an easy security in the "work of their hands," which are the gods they make for themselves. He is calling them to be faithful to the *Shema.* He promises: "I will heal their defection, I will love them freely, for my anger is turned away from them.... I will be like the dew to Israel, he shall blossom like the lily.... They will come and rest in my shadow, sprouting strong, like a stalk of corn.... Ephraim, what now to him his idols? I hear his prayer; it is I who keep his care. I blossom green like a cypress, on me his fruit is found" (Hos 14:4-9). God's love is calling for a return of love.

When, therefore, a scribe came up to Jesus and asked him, "Which commandment is first of all?" Jesus responded with the *Shema,* allowing this text to bear all that the prophets such as Hosea had found therein. However, he went on to add a famous phrase from Leviticus 19:18, and in so doing he opened up a new understanding of love:

> Jesus answered, "The first is, 'Hear, O Israel: The Lord our God, the Lord is one, and you shall love the Lord your God with all your heart, and with all your soul, and with all your mind, and with all your strength.' The second is this, 'You shall love your neighbor as yourself.' There is no other commandment greater than these."
>
> MARK 12:29-31, RSV

In joining these two commandments, Jesus has taught us the revolutionary truth that we must love God and each other with the same love and that we cannot separate these one from the other. The First Letter of John takes up this teaching, calling it a commandment of Jesus: "If any one says: 'I love God,' and hates his brother, he is a liar; for he who does not love his brother, whom he has seen, cannot love God whom he has not seen. And this commandment we have from him, that he who loves God should love his brother also" (1 Jn 4:20-21, RSV).

Our love for God is a return of love. It consists in allowing the love the Father has for us to take its place in our hearts and become a return of love to him. As St. Paul says: "The love of

God is poured out in our hearts through the Holy Spirit who was given to us" (Rom 5:5, RSV). Our love for our neighbor is part of this same movement of return to God. Recall here the statement of St. Augustine: "Love your neighbor, then look within yourself at the source of this love. There you will see, as far as you are able, God" (*Commentary on John's Gospel* 17, 8). In the same vein, St. Catherine of Siena once heard God tell her, "I have placed you in the midst of your brothers and sisters so that you can do for them what you cannot do for me. That is, you can love them freely without expecting any return."

Ask the Holy Spirit to show you how this teaching of Jesus—that the Father wishes us to love him and our brothers and sisters with the same love—applies to you today. With the light of the Holy Spirit also comes the power to implement what he reveals to us.

Saturday of the Third Week
Hosea 6:1-6; Luke 18:9-14

God tells us through the prophet Hosea today that he wants love, not sacrifice, and knowledge of God rather than holocausts. In the gospel Jesus tells us the parable about the Pharisee and the tax collector who both went to the temple to pray. If we penetrate the meaning of the two words "love" and "knowledge," we will enter into the heart of what Jesus is teaching us.

The Hebrew word from which we translate "love" in the passage from Hosea is one that many have heard about before: *hesed*. The word *hesed* describes an attitude, expressed in action, of an enthusiastic fidelity to a relationship. When God is described as "doing *hesed,*" the accent is often on the undeserved generosity with which he acts in fidelity to his promises and covenant. In this way, *hesed* may be translated as "mercy." When human beings show *hesed* they are responding to the demands of a relationship born of family, friendship, or covenant, and they do this generously and without hesitation. Perhaps Jesus' words in St. Matthew's Gospel show us the link between God's *hesed* and our *hesed:* "Blessed are the merciful, for mercy will be given to them [by God]" (Mt 5:7).

To "know God" is to recognize both him and his authority. To recognize God means being able to perceive his presence and come to know him intimately and affectionately. But this is not possible unless I also recognize—that is, acknowledge in my actions—his majesty and authority. This second aspect of knowing God is brought out clearly in these words of the Lord to King Jehoiakim:

> Woe to him who builds his house by unrighteousness, and his upper rooms by injustice; who makes his neighbor serve him for nothing, and does not give him his wages.... Do you think you are a king because you compete in cedar? Did not your father eat, drink, and do justice and righteousness? Then it was well with him. He judged the cause of the poor and needy; then it was well. Is not this to know me? says the Lord.
>
> JEREMIAH 22:13-16, RSV

The intimate link between knowing God and obeying him is stated more than once in the First Letter of John: "The one who claims, 'I know him,' while not keeping his commandments, is a liar, and the truth is not in him" (1 Jn 2:4). "Knowing God," therefore, signifies an intimate perception of him and a heart-felt and practical acknowledgement of his authority: these two cannot be separated.

Now let us apply these insights to the two men who "went up to the temple to pray." Luke tells us that Jesus directed the parable to those who "were self-confident, regarding themselves as upright and all others as contemptible." The first man took his stand and prayed regarding himself, thanking God that he was not like the rest of humanity "or even like this tax collector." The second man, the tax collector, stood far off and "would not even lift up his eyes to heaven, but beat his breast, saying, 'God, be merciful to me, a sinner!'" Jesus renders judgment in favor of the latter: "I tell you, this man went down to his house justified rather than the other."

The Pharisee was observant, but he lacked love, he lacked *hesed*. His obedience was not out of gratitude. Rather he presented it to God as achievement, something that guaranteed his acceptance, his justification, with God. The Pharisee also lacked knowledge of God. There was no intimacy in his prayer, no sense of responding to God's authority. Rather, his was a sense of self-congratulation.

The tax collector, on the other hand, out of his clear awareness of his need and of his true reality before God, never even looked up but only prayed for mercy, for *hesed*. Despite his sinful situation and his social ostracism, he knew that God would care for him and he had enough love to address himself to that. He had knowledge of God. Somehow he both perceived the Father's true character and wanted to submit himself to his authority. He went home justified.

If we learn to pray this way, we will come to experience the enthusiasm with which Jesus told this story. We will learn to stop praying, "I thank you that I am not like that Pharisee over there." We will finally and intimately entrust ourselves to the mercy of God.

CHAPTER FIVE

The Fourth Week of Lent
Receive the Light

※

Sunday of the Fourth Week
1 Samuel 16:1, 6-7, 10-13; Ephesians 5:8-14; John 9:1-41

Last Sunday set the theme of life-giving water, the Gift who is the Holy Spirit. The catechumens, and we with them, were offered the grace to thirst for this water. We prayed for them and for ourselves that we would be free of evil and able to rejoice in this gift.

This Sunday the theme is light. In the scrutiny prayer we ask to be brought into the truth:

Lord Jesus, you are the true light that enlightens the world. Through your Spirit of truth free those of us who in any way are enslaved by the father of lies. Stir up the desire for good in all of us whom you have chosen for your sacraments. Let us rejoice in your light, that we may see, and, like the man born blind whose sight you restored, let us prove to be staunch and fearless witnesses to the faith, for you are Lord for ever and ever. Amen.[1]

The truth is light, and we need light to see this light. Jesus, the true Light of the world—the Way, the Truth, and the Life—stood before the blind man, but his blindness prevented him from seeing Jesus. He needed light to see the light, and this Jesus gave him.

We are the same. We read in the Second Letter to the Corinthians: "The God who said, 'From darkness let light shine,' has caused light to shine in our hearts for the enlightenment which is the knowledge of the glory of God on the face of Jesus Christ" (2 Cor 4:6). The glory of God shines on the face of Jesus Christ even as I write this and you read it. The question is, do we see it? St. Paul says that God the Father, who at creation caused light to shine, has done an even greater work by causing light to shine in our hearts so that we can see his glory on the face of Christ.

We pray today and during the rest of Lent that at Easter we will be freed of our blindness, that we too will rise from our deadly somnolence and distraction and know Jesus more intimately and clearly. This is the meaning of the words in the second reading today: "Awake, O sleeper, and rise from the dead, and Christ will shine upon you" (Eph 5:14).

As we pray today that we will be freed from any enslavement caused by the Father of Lies, we see that this prayer of the Church is of great depth. Our slavery is to the lie, and our freedom comes from the Truth. And the greatest lie of our age is precisely concerning the true reality of God the Father, whose glory shines on the face of Jesus Christ. Jesus is the Truth precisely because he reveals the Father. This is the meaning of his whole life and death. He told Pilate: "For this I was born, for this I came into the world, that I might bear witness to the truth" (Jn 18:37, RSV).

Jesus Christ is the one who is "full of grace and truth." He has imparted these to us (see Jn 1:14, 17) by making the Father known. St. Paul describes the essential work of the Holy Spirit in very straightforward terms. He tells us it is precisely the work of the Spirit to bring about in our hearts that divine affection for the Father that was in the heart of Jesus: "That you are sons is manifest because God sent the Spirit of his Son into our hearts, crying Abba! Father! Thus you are no longer a slave but a son; if a son, then also an heir through God" (Gal 4:6-7; see the same teaching in Rom 8:14-17).

There is a lie that holds our age enslaved. It is based upon a conviction that is in direct opposition to the Trinitarian mission described by St. Paul in the Galatians text. This lie is at the root of teenage suicides; the tragedies of Auschwitz, Hiroshima, Kosovo, and Rwanda; and all the other inhumanities we experience and sometimes connive in. *It is the lie about God the Father* that says he is either uncaring or impotent. In this, the first civilization in history to be atheistic, we see the fruit of this lie. Pray today that you and your children will be set free from this enslavement by a revelation of the face of the Father.

While many people, because of past painful experiences, find the word *father* difficult, there is healing, even if it takes time. Through prayer, compassion, and, where necessary, genuine Christian counseling, the Truth who is Jesus will set us free. And we will rejoice in the glory of God the Father that shines on his face.

Monday of the Fourth Week

Isaiah 65:17-21; John 4:43-54

Many of the texts the Church has given us up to this point have been instructions that enable us to live our share in Christ's life more deeply. Some have revealed to us aspects of the Paschal Mystery, the death and resurrection of Christ, and a few have invited us into the sanctuary of his own inner life. From this point until Easter all the gospel texts will be from the Gospel of John, and they will serve to bring us more deeply into the mystery of Jesus' death and glorification. Today's texts begin this period with a prophecy that points to the meaning of Jesus' act of love on the cross and the fruit that this act will bear for us and for all of humanity.

Isaiah, or more likely someone in the "school" of Isaiah writing some two hundred years later, delivers a word of promise from the Lord. The message creates for us a symbolic understanding of what will be when God creates a "new heaven and a new earth." "Rejoice and be glad forever at what I create.... I will rejoice in Jerusalem and take delight in my people.... He dies a mere youth who lives but a hundred years.... They shall build houses and inhabit them; they shall plant vineyards and eat their fruit" (Is 65:18-21).

This prophecy is being fulfilled in Christ's creative work, the Church. The work was completed on the cross and in the Resurrection and sending of the Holy Spirit, but the full manifestation of that work awaits the moment when the new creation extends to the heavens and the earth and the new Jerusalem. What Isaiah prophesied was a shadow of what was to come; what we possess now in the time of the Church is the beginning fulfillment of that **prophecy** whose full glory is yet to be revealed.

John's Gospel shows us the life of Jesus fulfilling prophecy and being a prophecy of the life of the Church—that is, our life—until he returns. Today's account of Jesus' healing of the royal official's son is an example of this. Let us pay attention to the details of John's narrative and try to enter into what effect this action of Jesus, mediated to us by John's theological artistry, is meant to have in our lives.

First, Jesus is at Cana, "where he had made the water wine"—that is, where the splendid water of the old dispensation became the wine of the life of the Holy Spirit. John takes pains to point out to us that the healing of the official's son is "now the second sign that Jesus did when he had come from Judea to Galilee." The first sign was for the Jews, the second for the Gentiles. Then again, this is a healing at a distance, as are the other gospel miracles that have to do explicitly with non-Jews: those of the centurion's son and the daughter of the Syrophoenician woman.

When we reflect upon the meaning of these actions we can see, first, that Jesus, by this and other healings, has initiated the era prophesied by Isaiah. Second, we see that distance is no obstacle to him now. In this time of the Church, Jesus still heals and forgives "at a distance." That is, he may be absent in one way, but he is present in another. We should go to him as did the royal official, the centurion, and the foreign woman, and ask not only for ourselves but also for those who need to know his power experientially. The result of the healing narrated in today's gospel was that the royal official "believed, and all his household." Our answered prayers can have the same result.

Tuesday of the Fourth Week
Ezekiel 47:1-9, 12; John 5:1-16

Water is once again the symbolic theme of today's readings—water flowing from Christ's side and the water of Baptism. Both of these water images are expressions of the fruit of Jesus' death and resurrection.

The first reading is taken from one of the highlights of a long, nine-chapter description given by Ezekiel of what the land of Israel, and especially the temple, will be like when God restores his people. Typical of such prophetic visions is a certain mixing of horizons. We will concentrate on this first reading and then look at the gospel and its sequel tomorrow.

Ezekiel is speaking, immediately after the return of Israel from exile, about the promise of a restored temple; but he also describes in symbol what God will do when he makes good on all the promises he ever made to Israel. The prophet saw water flowing from the side of the new temple. It formed a stream that became progressively deeper until it was a mighty river flowing out into the desert and filling the Dead Sea. Then Ezekiel saw many trees along the banks of the river, and from the angel who accompanied him he heard of the life-giving power of this water:

> And wherever the river goes every living creature which swarms will live, and there will be very many fish; for this water goes there, that the waters of the sea may become fresh; so everything will live where the river goes.... And on the banks, on both sides of the river, there will grow all kinds of trees for food. Their leaves will not wither nor

their fruit fail, but they will bear fresh fruit every month, because the water for them flows from the sanctuary. Their fruit will be for food, and their leaves for healing.

EZEKIEL 47:9,12, RSV

Jesus is the new temple, and from his side flow rivers of living water. He prophesied,

"If any thirsts, let him come to me; and let the one who believes in me drink. As Scripture says [referring to the Ezekiel text among others]: 'From within him [Jesus] there will flow living water.'" Now he said this of the Spirit, which those who believed in him were going to receive. For the Spirit was not as yet [given to men] because Jesus had not yet been glorified [by his passion and resurrection].

JOHN 7:37-39

If we believe, we thirst; if we come to Jesus in faith, we will drink of the life-giving water, the Spirit, who flows from within him. John sets this forth again; he tells us that, as the soldier pierced Jesus' side on the cross, the place of Jesus' glorification, "suddenly there flowed out blood [his Passion] and water [the Holy Spirit]" (Jn 19:34). The sacraments were given to the Church at this moment when, as the new Adam slept, the new Eve—the Church—was born from his side. In the Preface of the Mass in honor of the Sacred Heart we hear: "Lifted high on the cross, Christ gave his life for us, so much did he love us. From his wounded side flowed blood and water, the fountain of sacramental life in the Church. To his open side the Savior invites all men to draw water in joy from the springs of salvation."[2]

Prayer:

Prayer:

Jesus, living temple, rock struck by Moses from which living water flows, we come to you thirsting for the refreshment that comes from your Spirit. Let us know the new life and new energy and joy that flow into us from your open side as we contemplate your love for us and taste the Holy Spirit.

✣

Wednesday of the Fourth Week
Isaiah 49:8-15; John 5:17-30

In yesterday's first reading Ezekiel gave us a prophecy of a new and restored Israel in symbols that were ultimately fulfilled in Jesus. Today Isaiah does the same. The word of the Lord through Isaiah promises a day of salvation, a time when prisoners will come forth, when a way will be cut through the mountains, and when the highway back from exile will be a level, easy road. Then, to encourage his people, the Lord adds: "But Zion said, 'The Lord has forsaken me, my Lord has forgotten me.' Can a woman forget her sucking child, that she should have no compassion on the son of her womb? Even these may forget, yet I will not forget you" (Is 49:14-15, RSV).

However, the gospel text today begins to sound an ominous note. It tells of the conflict stirred up by the healing miracle recorded in yesterday's reading. There we saw Jesus at the pool of Bethesda, a healing place with its five porticoes crowded with sick people of every description. One can still see this pool near the Church of St. Anne in Jerusalem. Jesus came to this desperate scene where humanity, not knowing to whom it should turn, was waiting for the waters to stir. He confronted one man who had been sick for thirty-eight years:

"Do you want to be healed?"

The sick man answered him, "Sir, I have no man to put me into the pool when the water is stirred, and while I am going another steps down before me."

Jesus said to him, "Rise, take up your pallet, and walk." And at once the man was healed, and he took up his pallet and walked.

JOHN 5:6-9, RSV

Salvation came, not by some chance stirring of the forces of this world but by the healing word of Jesus. The man, now healed and jubilant, was confronted by "the Jews," who demanded to know what kind of person would ever tell a man to carry his pallet on the Sabbath: "And this was why the Jews persecuted Jesus, because he did this on the Sabbath" (Jn 5:16, RSV). Thus began the conflict that continues today.

It is important to note that when John uses the phrase "the Jews," while he might be reflecting the actual historical actors in the life of Jesus, his is not a polemic against the people of the day. He is using the phrase as a symbolic way of designating all those who resist the truth, whether they are Jew or Gentile.

Jesus' answer to the Jews' accusation is a statement of his identity: "My Father is working still, and I am working." The Jews understood the significance of this response: "This was why the Jews sought all the more to kill him, because he not only broke the Sabbath but also called God his Father, making himself equal with God" (Jn 5:17-18, RSV). Jesus responds in a way that leads us into the heart of the mystery of the death and resurrection of *the Son of God*, for his earthly life realizes in a human dimension the selfless intimacy that he and the Father eternally enjoy in the unity of the Holy Spirit.

> Truly, truly, I say to you, the Son can do nothing of his own accord, but only what he sees the Father doing; for whatever he does, that the Son does likewise. For the Father loves the Son and shows him all that he himself is doing; and greater works than these will he show him, that you may marvel.... I can do nothing on my own authority; as I hear, I judge; and my judgment is just, because I seek not my own will but the will of him who sent me.
>
> JOHN 5:19-30, RSV

We now see that Jesus' human obedience is the reflection of his eternal relation to the Father, with whom he is completely equal and to whom he looks in love for everything. This is the secret of the power of his death. As he was on his way to Gethsemane, the prelude to his passion, he told his disciples that what he was going to face would not be a triumph of the Prince of this world but an expression of his love for and obedience to the Father: "But that the world might know that I love the Father; and as the Father commanded me, so I do— rise up, let us go from here" (Jn 14:31). This is the norm and source of our obedience.

Thursday of the Fourth Week
Exodus 32:7-14; John 5:31-47

In the first reading today from the Book of Exodus, we understand that Moses is a foreshadowing of Christ. In the gospel Jesus appeals to Moses as a witness to himself, while the Exodus passage shows us Moses as an intercessor. While he was on the mountain with God receiving the law that was to form God's people, the people were on the plain worshipping the golden calf and thus breaking the very first and most fundamental commandment, "You shall have no other gods besides me" (Ex 20:3).

God tells Moses to "leave him alone" so that he can destroy the people who have sinned. But Moses knows what God is really saying. Later, through the mouth of Ezekiel, the Lord says: "And I sought for a man among them who should build up the wall and stand in the breach before me for the land, that I should not destroy it; but I found none" (Ez 22:30, RSV). Here God does find one who, like Christ, will stand in the breach and save the people: "So the Lord relented in the punishment he had threatened to inflict on his people" (Ex 32:14).

Parents, intercede for your children; pastors, intercede for your people; teachers, for your students; everyone, intercede for the world by the power of the cross of Christ. Stand in the breach, like Moses and like Jesus, as an instrument of salvation for the people close to you.

To the Jews who took exception to Jesus' calling himself God's Son and making himself equal to God, Jesus first responded, as we heard yesterday, with a description of his relation to the Father. Today the gospel gives us the second part of that response, namely Jesus' appeal to witnesses. In answer to a supposed objection that in describing his relation to the Father Jesus is testifying on his own behalf, he invokes four witnesses: John the Baptist, the works the Father gave him to accomplish, the Father himself, and the Scriptures, especially the Law of Moses.

Testimony evokes belief or disbelief, yet believing is part of the human condition. In the encyclical *Faith and Reason* (31), Pope John Paul II describes this fact of human existence: "Who in the end could forge anew the paths of experience and thought which have yielded the treasures of human wisdom and religion? This means that the human being—the one who seeks the truth—is also *the one who lives by belief*."

It is important, then, that we receive and yield to the testimony offered in regard to the divine nature of Jesus, since the heart of our faith is the acknowledgement that "Jesus is Lord." The witness of the Baptist is the witness of the last prophet of the Old Testament, a man sent by God who can tell us that Jesus has been sent by the Father. Jesus is still performing works; in fact, he tells us, "Believe me: I am in the Father and the Father in me. If not, believe because of the works" (Jn 14:11).

Look at your life, and the life of the whole Church, and consider the answers to prayer that you know you have received from Jesus. Think, "Who is this who answers prayer?" and believe because of the works.

The testimony of the Father is constant. Through the Holy Spirit he is always speaking to our conscience, leading us to yield more profoundly to the Truth that is Jesus: "No one comes to me unless the Father who sent me draws him" (Jn 6:44, RSV).

Finally, the Scriptures, in this case the Old Testament, bear witness to Jesus. Reflect on the story of Moses today. Can you not see there an anticipation of what Jesus accomplished by dying out of love and obedience and in solidarity with us? Who then is this Jesus who can confer a likeness to himself even before he comes among us? He is the Son of the living God who is himself "the faithful witness, the firstborn of the dead, the ruler of kings on earth" (Rv 1:5, RSV).

None of these witnesses will force you to acknowledge who Jesus Christ really is. If only you will allow yourself to be freely led by their testimony, you will come to know for yourself that Jesus Christ, the one who died and rose for us, who won the right to give us the Holy Spirit and eternal life, is the Son of God.

⚜

Friday of the Fourth Week
Wisdom 2:1, 12-22; John 7:1-2, 10, 25-30

There is a text in the Gospel of John that summarizes well what the readings of today's liturgy are teaching us: "This is the judgment: the light has come into the world and men loved the darkness rather than the light, for their works were evil. For everyone carrying out evil hates the light, and does not come to the light, so that his works be not exposed. The one doing the truth comes to the light so that his works be manifest because they have been done in God" (Jn 3:19-21).

Darkness hates the light, and when our deeds are dark we do everything we can to stay away from the light and even to extinguish the light itself. The words of the evildoers in the Book of Wisdom, which we hear today, give voice to this principle. They find the "just one" unbearable because his very life as well as his words are an affront to them: "He became to us a reproof of our thoughts; the very sight of him is a burden to us, because his manner of life is unlike that of others, and his ways are strange" (Wis 2:14-15, RSV). This comes to such a pass that they decide to extinguish the light itself:

> Let us see if his words are true, and let us test what will happen at the end of his life; for if the just one is God's son, he will help him, and will deliver him from the hand of his adversaries. Let us test him with insult and torture that we may find out how gentle he is, and make trial of his forbearance. Let us condemn him to a shameful death, for, according to what he says, he will be protected.
>
> WISDOM 2:17-20, RSV

It is with great spiritual insight therefore that St. Matthew's Gospel expresses the insults at the cross in such a way that we see, in the allusion to the Wisdom text, the same opposition to light. In both texts it is the same principle at work: "He trusts in God; let God deliver him now, if he desires him; for he said, 'I am the Son of God'" (Mt 27:43, RSV).

Twice in the gospel text we read that "the Jews" were "trying to kill" Jesus, and once that "they tried to arrest him." This is the same opposition to the just one described for us in the Book of Wisdom. However, at the very center of the gospel passage is a debate among the inhabitants of Jerusalem concerning where Jesus comes from: he cannot be the Messiah because they know his origins. Jesus responds with another affirmation of his relation to the Father: "Yes, you know me and you know where I am from, but I have not come on my own accord. Rather, there is One who is true who sent me whom you do not know. I know him because I am from him and he sent me" (Jn 7:28-29).

It is as if Jesus were saying, "You know something of my human origins, but my real identity and my real origin are hidden from you. I am from the Father, the true One, I am one with him and yet he is my Origin. You do not know this because you too resist the light by which it is revealed. If you knew this you would understand the true significance of my death for you."

These words are addressed to us. Do we ourselves really *know* who Jesus is? Do we understand the death of him who from all eternity is equal to the Father and proceeds from him? In this awareness, which is a gift of the Holy Spirit, we find the true meaning of our own life, and we come to an intimacy with Jesus, the Son of God. Do you yearn for this?

Observe the way in which we are brought to the place of revelation: "The one who has my commandments and keeps them is the one who loves me, and the one who loves me will be loved by my Father, and I will love him and *reveal myself to him*" (Jn 14:21). Listen to Jesus and obey him, and he will bring you to the place where he reveals to you himself and his love, and you will know the love of the Father. Make this the practice of a lifetime, and you will have joy and have it in abundance.

Saturday of the Fourth Week
Jeremiah 11:18-20; John 7:40-53

Once again Jeremiah's words open for us some secrets of the soul of Jesus. The Lord has made known to Jeremiah the plans of his enemies. Before that, as he says, "I was like a lamb led trustingly to the slaughter. I did not know it was against me that they were devising schemes saying, 'Let us destroy the tree while the sap is in it; let us cut him off from the land of the living, that his name be remembered no more.'" Jeremiah then prays to the "Just Judge, the searcher of minds and hearts," and asks to see vengeance taken on them, "for to you I have made known my complaint" (Jer 11:18-20).

Postponing for the moment our reflection on Jeremiah's prayer for redress, let us try to enter into the sacramental power of his prayer in reaction to the betrayal and suffering being prepared for him. There we can see, even if only imperfectly, a foreshadowing of the suffering of Jesus, who knew what awaited him. Jesus could see himself as a lamb being led to the slaughter, and this rejection and lack of love, this hatred of the light, filled him with great sadness.

Far more than Jeremiah, Jesus knew how much those who were plotting his death ran the risk of depriving themselves of the eternal life he came to restore to humanity. His sadness was a human sadness. As St. Jerome expresses it: "Our Lord, to prove the truth of the manhood he had assumed, experiences real sadness" (*On Matthew 26:27*). To appreciate this sadness is to be purified of sin and to grow in likeness to Jesus, who has promised: "Blessed are they who mourn, they shall be consoled" (Mt 5:4).

There are three things to bear in mind when considering Jeremiah's prayer for justice. First, Jeremiah knows that God is just, he is the Just Judge, and he will punish those who plot murder and carry it out. Secondly, Jeremiah sees that his death will mean that the word of God entrusted to him, which has caused him so much suffering, will no longer be available to the people whom he loves so much. Thirdly, in other places Jeremiah prays for his enemies: "I swear, O Lord, that I have served you for their good, I have interceded with you in time of trouble and misfortune: you know I have" (Jer 15:11).

This third point teaches that a prayer for justice is not always a prayer of anger and revenge. The proof of this particular kind of justice can be seen in the prayer of those slain for their Christian faith: "O Lord, holy and true, how long will you not judge and avenge our blood on the inhabitants of the earth?" (Rv 6:10). This too is not a prayer for personal satisfaction at seeing one's persecutors punished, but a plea that God manifest *his* justice as he sees fit.

Again, we read after the parable of the insistent widow who finally prevails upon the unjust judge: "Will not God obtain the rights of his chosen ones who cry out to him day and night? Will he delay long over them? I tell you, he will give them justice soon enough. But when the Son of Man comes will he find faith [prayer and an understanding of *God's* justice] on the earth?" (Lk 18:7-8).

Justice is not served by making light of wrongdoing, but it is brought to a divine perfection in forgiveness. The proof of this principle of God's justice is made manifest in the cross of Christ, of which we sing in the famous Easter hymn, the Exultet: "Father, how wonderful your care for us! How boundless your merciful love! To ransom a slave you gave away your

Son. O happy fault, O necessary sin of Adam, which gained for us so great a redeemer!"[3]

When God forgave us through the death and resurrection of his Son, he knew what he was forgiving, and yet he willingly provided for us. That is the perfection of justice, a justice that looks to the person and not only the wrong committed. This is the type of justice we saw in the parents who forgave the murderers of their children at Littleton. They knew that they had suffered injustice, yet they chose to imitate the justice of God and forgive. We should all look into our hearts and pray for this capacity to imitate God's loving and merciful pardon.

CHAPTER SIX

The Fifth Week of Lent
The Promise of Life

✺
Sunday of the Fifth Week
Ezekiel 37:12-14; Romans 8:8-11; John 11:1-45

Life is so mysterious and so precious. This Sunday as we, both baptized and catechumens, prepare each in our own way for the feast of Life, which is now only two weeks away, the Church gives us the Sunday of life. The readings all speak of this life, the scrutiny prays for it, and the Creed presented to the catechumens as part of their formation ends with an act of faith in "the resurrection of the body and the life of the world to come."

We are meant to experience already the fact that we are called and destined by God for eternal life. This means that we will be totally transformed, body and soul, for all eternity because of the gift that the Trinity makes of himself to us. The gift is made to us as we are, a self-conscious union of body and soul. It is what Pope John Paul II calls "subjectivity":

... Divinization is to be understood not only as an interior state of man (that is, of the subject) capable of seeing

God face to face, but also as a new formation of the whole personal subjectivity of man in accordance with union with God in his Trinitarian mystery, and of intimacy with him in the perfect communion of persons. This intimacy—with all its subjective intensity—will not absorb man's personal subjectivity, but rather will make it stand out to an incomparably greater and fuller extent.[1]

General Audience of December 9, 1981

This is an example of God's "humanism"—his love for humankind.

In chapter five of St. John's Gospel, Jesus promises that "the hour is coming and now is, when the dead will hear the voice of the Son of God and those who hear will live" (Jn 5:25, RSV). In the gospel today Jesus raises Lazarus back to this life. In so doing he provides a symbolic anticipation of that future moment when those who are joined to him will hear his voice and rise, body and soul, to share in the divine life. As he promises elsewhere, "This is the will of my Father: that all who look on the Son and believe in him should have eternal life, and I will raise him up on the last day.... I am the living bread come down from heaven; if anyone eats of this bread, he will live forever; and the bread that I will give is my flesh for the life of the world" (Jn 6:40, 51).

The gospel today tells us how Jesus, knowing that Lazarus is sick, still waits and then announces, "Our friend Lazarus has fallen asleep, but I go to awake him out of sleep" (Jn 11:11, RSV). Once he arrives there, Martha, Lazarus' sister, comes out to him. Jesus tells her, "Your brother will rise again." She expresses her Jewish faith in a general resurrection of all the faithful dead, but Jesus responds: "I am the resurrection and the life; he who believes in me, though he die, yet shall he live, and whoever lives and believes in me shall never die. Do you believe this?"

Martha makes an act of faith in Jesus. Mary comes to join them. At the tomb Jesus begins to weep, and then Lazarus hears the voice of Jesus: "Lazarus, come out!" The dead man comes out. This is what Jesus will do for all those who are dead in sin if they will let themselves hear his voice. Our resurrection must begin in this life if it is to be completed in the next.

For this reason the prayer of exorcism that accompanies the third scrutiny asks for new life. The prayer is for the catechumens, but it can be adapted to apply to us all:

> Lord Jesus, by raising Lazarus from the dead you showed that you came that we might have life and have it more abundantly. Free from the grasp of death both those who await your life-giving sacraments and those of us who have already received them, and deliver us from the spirit of corruption. Through your Spirit, who gives life, fill us with faith, hope, and charity that we may live with you always in the glory of your resurrection, for you are Lord for ever and ever. Amen.[2]

Monday of the Fifth Week
Daniel 13:1-9, 15-17, 19-30, 33-62; John 8:1-11

The theme of today's readings may be termed "salvation by wisdom." We hear how the youth Daniel saved Susanna from a false accusation of adultery and how Jesus saved a woman who had committed adultery. We are meant to see how our own salvation from all the consequences of our sins has been brought about through the wisdom of God, who sent his Son to die and rise for us.

But there is more. Scholars point out that in the early days of the Church at Rome, the liturgy began in one church, called a "station church," and then went in procession (really more like a parade) to another. On the way the people sang, the readings were proclaimed, and the celebrant preached. Thus, the readings were meant for all passersby to hear as the procession made its way through the city.

The readings we have today were originally connected with the station church of St. Susanna, built in honor of a Roman martyr but also evoking the Susanna of our first reading. This church, which still stands, was located in the red-light district of Rome. The message is twofold: God protects chastity; and everyone who comes into contact with Jesus can be saved from their sin.

In the first reading Daniel saves Susanna from the vicious accusations of two lecherous old men who want to punish her for not yielding to their wishes. In the gospel reading Jesus saves a woman from those who merely want to use her and her sin as a means to trap Jesus and discredit him. His wisdom and mercy humiliate them.

That we possess this gospel story is due to a special act of the Holy Spirit. It is an example of a "floating" narrative, most often found as an insertion in John's Gospel at a place where it serves as another example of Jesus' teaching in the temple area. Other manuscripts place it in a similar place in Luke (after Luke 21:38) or at the end of Luke or John. This cameo, revealing the compassion and courage of Jesus, is one of the small treasures found in the Scriptures.

It is early in the morning, and Jesus is sitting in the temple area preparing to teach.

> The scribes and the Pharisees brought a woman who had been caught in adultery, and placing her in the midst they said to him, "Teacher, this woman has been caught in the act of adultery. Now in the law Moses commanded us to stone such. What do you say about her?" This they said to test him, that they might have some charge to bring against him.
>
> JOHN 8:3-6, RSV

By stating that the woman was "caught," her accusers are implying that there were two witnesses. They invoke the Law of Moses, but the Law required that both parties to the adultery be punished. It is clear that in this Jesus' enemies were placing Jesus in a dilemma: should he agree with the Law and contradict his own message of the Father's mercy, or should he contradict the Law and expose himself to the charge of lawlessness? He stooped and wrote on the ground. Was he merely ignoring them or pausing for thought, or was he writing something? If it is the latter, then the best guess is Jeremiah 17:13, "Those who forsake you shall be written on the dirt, for they have forsaken the Lord, the fountain of living water." Jesus is hinting at the guilt of the woman's accusers.

Finally Jesus straightens up and confronts the malice of these men who are only too happy to destroy the woman in order to get at him: "The man among you who has no sin, let him be the first to cast a stone at her." He continues to write on the ground while, one by one, they go away, "beginning with the eldest." Jesus and the woman are left alone, "mercy and misery," as St. Augustine expresses it. Jesus looks up: "Woman, where are they? Has no one condemned you?" She says, "No one, Lord." And Jesus says, "Neither do I condemn you; go, and do not sin again."

Let these words echo in your heart until you see the face of mercy.

❧

Tuesday of the Fifth Week
Numbers 21:4-9; John 8:21-30

The readings today bring us into the mystery of the cross. On the cross Jesus is "lifted up," both in the sense that he is hoisted on the cross and in the sense that he is glorified in this act with a glory that he possesses even now.

The story in the Book of Numbers is one of a series of narratives about the desert wanderings in which we see the rhythm of sin—punishment—repentance—forgiveness—restoration. In this case the people murmur—once again. Exasperated and tired of eating only manna, they "complain against God and Moses."

God is bringing these poor escaped slaves into a land that will be their own. There they will meet with him, know his presence and his care, and become a prosperous nation. Yet they trust him so little that they cannot accept his provision: "Why have you brought us up out of Egypt to die in the wilderness where there is no food and no water? We are disgusted with this miserable food" (Nm 21:5).

In punishment, God sends venomous serpents among the people, and many die. Then the Israelites acknowledge their sin and beg Moses to ask God to take away the serpents. Moses prays, and God replies: "'Make a serpent, and lift it up on a pole; and everyone who is bitten, when he sees it, shall live.' So Moses made a bronze serpent, and lifted it up on a pole; and if a serpent bit any man, he would look at the bronze serpent and live" (Nm 21:8-9).

In looking upon the exalted image of what their sins deserve, the people are saved from death. This is what Jesus said earlier in John's Gospel: "And as Moses lifted up the serpent in the wilderness, so must the Son of man be lifted up, that whoever believes in him may have eternal life" (Jn 3:14-15, RSV). Jesus on the cross portrays what our sins deserve. And yet if we gaze upon him with faith, we are healed, and we have eternal life: "When I am lifted up from the earth, I will draw everyone to myself" (Jn 12:32, RSV).

The reason for this rhythm of salvation is found in the unfathomable union between Jesus and the Father. In the gospel today Jesus once again speaks of his relation to the Father to answer his opponents' objections and to reveal the source of the power of his death and resurrection. His opponents finally ask him, "Who are you?" and Jesus replies, "What I told you at the beginning," and then goes on to speak of their condemnation. They still do not understand, so Jesus states clearly: "When you lift up the Son of Man, then you will know that I AM, and that of myself I do nothing, but I speak as the Father taught me. And he who sent me is with me; he has not left me alone because I always do what is pleasing to him" (Jn 8:28-29).

If we gaze on Jesus lifted up on the cross, exalted by the will of the Father, we experience in ourselves the saving and healing effects of this portrayal of our sins borne by Jesus out of love. Because he does nothing except what he sees the Father doing, we know that the authority and power of his death is divine. Therefore we know that he bears the sacred name, I AM.

God told Moses this name so that Moses could tell the Israelites who had sent him: "I AM WHO I AM.... Say this to the people of Israel, 'I AM has sent me to you'" (Ex 3:14, RSV). In contrast to Moses, Jesus bears the same name as the Father who sent him, for they are one. From all eternity they had agreed on this divine plan of mercy. In carrying it out, Jesus is doing what is pleasing to the Father. This is his glorification and the revelation of the Father's love: "God so loved the world that he gave his only Son, that whoever believes in him should not perish but have eternal life" (Jn 3:16, RSV).

> O immeasurably tender love! Who would not be set afire with such love? What heart could keep from breaking? You, deep well of charity, it seems you are so madly in love with your creatures that you could not live without us!...What could move you to such mercy? Neither duty nor any need you have of us (we are sinful and wicked debtors!)—but only love.[3]
>
> St. Catherine of Siena

꽃

Wednesday of the Fifth Week
Daniel 3:14-20, 91-92, 95; John 8:31-42

The narrative in the Book of Daniel tells us about three young Jewish men who obeyed God and refused to worship a statue of King Nebuchadnezzar. The king sought to punish them by having them thrown into a fiery furnace, but God delivered them. In the midst of the fire the king saw not three but four young men—"the fourth looks like a son of God"—and they were singing and praising God. When he saw this, Nebuchadnezzar blessed the God of Shadrach, Meshach, and Abednego, "who sent his angel to deliver those who trust in him" (Dn 3:28).

If we are attentive, we can see that the Church has placed this account here because it is a foreshadowing of the way in which the Father vindicated Jesus. This is the beloved Son who obeyed his Father right through death and was thus, through resurrection, delivered from death for his sake and ours: "Son though he was, he learned obedience from what he suffered; and being made perfect, he became for all who obey him the source of eternal salvation" (Heb 5:8-9).

The gospel shows us still another conflict situation between Jesus and "the Jews." In the portion of the text we have today, Jesus invites those Jews who have begun to believe in him to become his disciples and enter into the way of freedom: "If you abide in my word you are truly my disciples, and you will know the truth, and the truth will set you free." His interlocutors, willing only to consider an external freedom, reply that they are the sons of Abraham and thus are slaves to no one. Jesus replies, "Amen, amen, I tell you, everyone who does sin is a slave of sin.... If, however, the Son sets you free, you are free indeed." He goes on to point out to them that they are looking for a chance to kill him, "because my word finds no place with you" (Jn 8:31-37).

The importance of this text for us is that it not only points to the deep source of resistance on the part of "the Jews" who are trying to kill Jesus but also confronts us with the source of our own resistance to him. We become disciples by having the word of Jesus "abide" in us. This term describes a very intense and inner activity, initiated and sustained by the Holy Spirit, by which we allow the Word of Jesus to have its effect within us. The Word itself, anointed by the Holy Spirit, has energy to change us, to lead us out of sin into the light if we will "abide" in it. St. Paul speaks of the same mystery when he tells the Thessalonians that the Word "is at work in you," making them imitators of the churches who are standing firm in persecution (see 1 Thes 2:13-14).

Jesus tells us that as we become truly disciples, we will know the truth, and the truth will set us free. Jesus is the Truth. As we abide in his Word, we come to discover Jesus in progressively deeper ways, and thus we understand that he himself is the very revelation of the Father. The self-revelation of the truth, the knowledge of the Father in the Son—this is what sets us free. That such is the case is clear from Jesus' own words that follow: "If the *Son* sets you free, you are free indeed." The way to freedom is in yielding to the interior action of the Holy Spirit as he brings the Word of Jesus alive in us. This Word brings us into contact with Jesus himself—"You will know the truth"—and Jesus is the very image of the Father—"The one who has seen me has seen the Father" (Jn 14:9, RSV).

Jesus is most himself on the cross: it is there that we can see his love for the Father. His pierced heart is the place where we can see, in human dimensions, the immense and eternal love between the Father and the Son. When we remember that, since the Resurrection, Jesus is fixed in the act of love in which he died, we can understand how abiding in his Word brings us to know him in ever more intimate ways. Then we discover that by his very being he is the revelation of the Father. Pray today and for the rest of Lent for the precious gift of that obedience to the Word of Jesus Christ, which will bring you to freedom.

Thursday of the Fifth Week
Genesis 17:3-9; John 8:51-59

Through the Gospel of John the Church continues to lead us into the hidden depths of the Paschal Mystery. The very foundation of St. John's theology of the Passion and Resurrection is to be found in the identity of Jesus Christ, in his divine Sonship, his complete and eternal union with the Father.

The reading from Genesis today is meant to remind us of the greatness of Abraham, our father in faith. This in turn helps us appreciate the significance of Jesus' claim in his ongoing controversy with "the Jews" that "before Abraham was, I AM." The Genesis text records for us the reiteration of God's covenant promise to Abram. God appears to Abram (that was his name then) and tells him: "Walk before me and be wholehearted with me." He mentions once again the covenant he has already made with Abram to make him the father of a countless progeny.

Abram bows to the ground, and God changes his name from Abram ("My Father—that is, God—is exalted") to Abraham ("the father of a multitude"). When a change of name is divinely given, then someone's whole life takes a new direction. That person has a new mission. Think of Simon, who became Peter. Our names, too, given at baptism and confirmation can be significant.

Abraham is the father of all who believe; in the liturgy we call him "our father in faith" (Canon I). Rightly then do the Jewish people honor this man who is at the origin of their race and the first to believe. We realize now that the "progeny" in whom the entire world is blessed is Jesus Christ. All who have faith in him share in his life and are the children of Abraham: "Know, then, that the people of faith, these are children of Abraham. Scripture, foreseeing that God justifies the gentiles from faith, proclaimed the gospel beforehand to Abraham: 'All the gentiles will be blessed in you.' So, then, the people of faith are blessed along with the believing Abraham" (Gal 3:7-9).

When Jesus says, "Whoever keeps my word will never die," his opponents object: Abraham and all the prophets died, just who do you make yourself out to be? Once again Jesus appeals to the witness of the Father: "If I glorify myself, my glory is nothing; it is my Father who glorifies me, of whom you say that he is your God." He goes on to add, "Your father Abraham rejoiced that he was to see my day; he saw it and was glad."

In the Jewish tradition the promise and even more the presence of Isaac (whose name alludes to laughter) was the means by which Abraham saw the fulfillment of the promise yet to come. Jesus is claiming that, in that prophetic intuition, Abraham dimly saw Jesus' "day" and "was glad." "The Jews" reason that if Abraham saw this fulfillment, then Jesus must have somehow already existed. They object that Jesus, born less than fifty years before, could not have been present to Abraham. Jesus reveals more of his identity: "Amen, amen, I say to you that before Abraham even existed, I AM." And they try to kill him.

We have already considered the source of the expression "I AM." It is, in the biblical tradition, a divine name that expresses God's eternal existence: "Say this to the people of Israel, 'I AM has sent me to you'" (Ex 3:14, RSV). Years later, an inspired theologian—the man responsible for the second part of the Book of Isaiah—opened up some of the potential of this ineffable name. For instance, we may translate Isaiah 51:1 as, "My people shall know my name; in that day (they shall know) that

I AM is the one who speaks." In describing himself as "I AM," Jesus is claiming once again that "the Father and I are one" (Jn 10:30).

Now look once again at the cross and see who it is who died for you. The depths of this mystery are beyond us, but we are invited to cross the threshold and begin to experience something of the fire of love within the Trinity. This love, through the cross, gathers us up in the movement of life between the Father, the Son, and the Holy Spirit.

⚜

Friday of the Fifth Week
Jeremiah 20:10-13; John 10:31-42

Jeremiah, in his life and words, is once again the living prophecy of the Suffering Messiah. "For I hear many whispering, there is terror on every side! 'Denounce him! Let us denounce him!' All my familiar friends are watching for my fall." Evil, enmity, and terror surround the just man. Yet he knows "the Lord is with me as a dread warrior; therefore my persecutors will stumble, they will not overcome me. They will be greatly shamed." Then once again Jeremiah prays for God's justice and looks forward to the moment when God will deliver him: "Sing to the Lord; praise the Lord! For he has delivered the life of the needy from the hand of evildoers" (Jer 20:10-13, RSV).

Jesus was familiar with these words and he knew their truth. He knew the suffering that awaited him, and he had confidence that the Father would deliver him. This is the mystery, the human suffering of the Son of God. He is one with the

115

Father, and yet he can know fear and loneliness. There is no one lonely and afraid, no one persecuted and in dread of great suffering, who is a stranger to Jesus. The person dying alone, someone in prison tortured and mocked, the mother with a sick child, the father who fears for his family, the old, the sick, the homeless, the abandoned and abused: Jesus understands them all; he has passed this way.

We can minister to this pain of Christ by reaching out to those who, at this moment, are experiencing it: "Whatever you did for the least of my brethren you did for me" (Mt 25:40-41). This, as we have seen, is an essential part of Lent, and indeed of the Christian life.

The gospel selection for today is taken from chapter ten of St. John's Gospel rather than chapter seven, which we have been hearing. But the conflict remains the same. "The Jews" resist Jesus' self-revelation and want to kill him. They claim to be ready to stone Jesus not because of his works "but for blasphemy; because you, being a man, make yourself God."

Jesus responds with a verse from Psalm 82, "I say, 'You are gods, sons of the Most High, all of you'" (Ps 82:6, RSV). In the psalm these words are addressed to judges who enjoy high status. They are told that, because of their sins, "yet you shall die and fall like any other prince." In the Jewish tradition, however, these words are believed to have been spoken to the people of Israel when the Word of God was addressed to them at Sinai. That is why Jesus goes on, "If he called them gods to whom the Word of God came (and Scripture cannot be set aside), do you say of him whom the Father sanctified and sent into the world, 'You are blaspheming,' because I said, 'I am the Son of God'?" If receiving the word of God makes someone a "god" and a "son of the Most High," then how much more is he the Son of God who, in the depths of his being, is the very Person of the Word of God himself? It is he who has been sent by the Father into the world to save it.

Jesus' second response is linked to the first. Anyone who has eyes to see can perceive that what Jesus is doing and will do is rooted in his union with the Father: "If I am not doing the works of my Father, then do not believe me; but if I do them, even though you do not believe me, believe the works, that you may know and understand that the Father is in me and I am in the Father" (Jn 10:37-38, RSV). We are meant to understand that his imminent death and resurrection are among the "works of the Father" that clearly show the identity of Jesus. That means that we, who receive the fruit of these acts in a daily and present way, are enabled to perceive who Jesus really is and confess his name to the world: These works enable us to "know and understand that the Father is in me and I am in the Father." This brings us to experience the truth that "whoever confesses that Jesus is the Son of God, God abides in him and he in God" (1 Jn 4:15, RSV).

Saturday of the Fifth Week
Ezekiel 37:1-28; John 11:45-56

On this, the last day before Holy Week, the Church combines in a dramatic way two themes that have been present all through Lent. There is first the royal majesty of Jesus, the living Son of God, and there is as well the growing intensity of the opposition to Jesus and the plot of the leaders to kill him. Both of these themes are found in the Ezekiel text, in which

God promises to gather his people from their exile and to establish his king, the Son of David.

> Behold, I will take the people of Israel from the nations among which they have gone, and will gather them from all sides, and bring them to their own land; and I will make them one nation in the land.... I will save them from all the backslidings in which they have sinned, and will cleanse them; and they shall be my people, and I will be their God. My servant David shall be king over them; and they shall all have one shepherd.... Then the nations will know that I the Lord sanctify Israel, when my sanctuary is in the midst of them for evermore.
>
> EZEKIEL 37:21-28, RSV

The deliberations of the "chief priests and Pharisees" in the gospel account are the study of a darkened mind. Having heard of the reaction of the crowd to the raising of Lazarus and Jesus' other wonders, these leaders are threatened. They reason: "What are we to do? For this man performs many signs. If we let him go on like this, everyone will believe in him, and the Romans will come and destroy both our holy place and our nation."

It is then that Caiaphas speaks up, saying more than he realizes: "You know nothing at all; you do not understand that it is expedient for you that one man should die for the people, and that the whole nation should not perish" (Jn 11:47-50). Caiaphas' solution is to hand Jesus over and have him executed. Thus the Jews will show themselves to be loyal subjects; also they will rid themselves of someone they detest and who possibly could raise up a following large enough in the eyes of the Romans to implicate the nation.

Caiaphas unwittingly gives expression to God's plan. John explains that because Caiaphas was high priest that fateful year, he "prophesied that Jesus should die for the nation, and not for the nation only, but to gather into one the children of God who are scattered abroad" (Jn 11:51-52, RSV).

The new David would die "for the nation, and not for the nation only," and he would gather together not only scattered Israel but all "the dispersed children of God." Thus Ezekiel's prophecy is abundantly fulfilled and Caiaphas' ironic prophecy is achieved through the death of Jesus. This reflects the prophecy of Jesus himself: "The Son of Man came not to be served but to serve and to give his life as a ransom for many" (Mk 10:45, RSV).

We are the many who have been gathered from the four corners of the world to form a new people. We are those who give glory to the Father for his saving work through the cross of Jesus Christ.

CHAPTER SEVEN

Holy Week and Easter
The Paschal Mystery

The whole of the Paschal Mystery is concentrated in that one moment in which Our Lord Jesus Christ, in an act of immeasurably great and intense love, died in a gift of himself to the Father for us. That moment still exists in the glorious humanity of Christ, and it is into that act that we are baptized: we are baptized into his death (see Rom 6:3). The Eucharist is the presence of this glorious Lord inviting us to share in his act of love, feeding us on his transformed Body and Blood, forming us into his Body, and giving us a share in his own life. "The one who eats my body and drinks my blood has eternal life, and I will raise him up on the last day" (Jn 6:54, RSV).

While the whole of the liturgy refracts the otherwise blinding white light of that act of love, Holy Week, with its concentration on the mystery, is a particularly privileged moment of grace. The early Christians in fact celebrated in one all-night vigil what we now celebrate in the course of a week. The custom of dividing aspects of this one Paschal Mystery began in Jerusalem. There pilgrims could go from site to site and commemorate in turn the entry into Jerusalem, the Last Supper and arrest, the trial, the Crucifixion and burial, and finally the Resurrection. This seventeen-hundred-year-old liturgical custom, now existing in nearly all Christian observances, has unfolded such riches that even the long Lenten preparation for this week can hardly begin to plumb their depths. In the short meditations that follow, we will keep our eyes fixed on the heart of the Paschal Mystery as the Church presents it to us.

✻

Palm Sunday of the Lord's Passion
Matthew 21:1-11 (Procession); Isaiah 50:4-7;
Philippians 2:6-11; Matthew 26:14–27:66 (Passion Narrative)

The first act of the Holy Week liturgy is to greet Jesus as he enters his city to be crowned king through his passion and resurrection. Already the gospel text speaks of his entrance into Jerusalem in terms that are redolent of a *parousia*—the arrival of an emperor in a triumphant victory parade with songs of celebration and welcome. In thus commemorating this past event in the life of Jesus, we are at the same time expressing our faith that "he will come again in glory to judge the living and the dead." It is then that the entire world will understand the meaning of what transpired that day in Jerusalem. Jesus, in an anticipatory symbolic act, declared his Messiahship by entering Jerusalem. He came to fulfill all that the Father willed his Messiah to accomplish on the way to becoming king. This faith vision is meant to illumine our understanding of Jesus' journey, through the abasement and pain of the cross, to his present state at God's right hand.

After the procession with palms we listen to three readings. The first, from Isaiah, is one of the four oracles or Songs of the Servant found in the latter chapters of that book. We will begin to reflect on these tomorrow.

The second reading is probably an ancient hymn quoted by St. Paul to help the Philippians understand the deep source of the radiant light that is at the center of the Church and the source of its unity. This reading forms the leitmotif of Holy Week as it traces the whole rhythm of the Paschal Mystery, beginning from Jesus' eternal and equal status with the Father on through his incarnation, passion, and death. The mystery culminates in the Lord's exaltation and the final recognition of his true identity. Let us follow this rhythm closely:

> Christ Jesus, while being in the form of God, did not consider being equal to God something to be clutched at. Rather he emptied himself, taking the form of a slave, being born in human likeness and in appearance found as a man. He humbled himself, becoming obedient, unto death on a cross. Therefore God raised him on high and gave to him the Name that is above every name; so that at this name of Jesus every knee should bow of those in heaven, on earth, and under the earth, and every tongue confess that Jesus Christ is Lord, to the glory of God the Father.
>
> PHILIPPIANS 2:6-11

Bear this text in your heart during Holy Week. You will see who it is who has died for you. The One who is in the very nature of God, equal to God the Father, in an act of unimaginable humility, somehow without ceasing to be who he is, emptied himself and came among us as a man indistinguishable from the rest of us. Then, in obedience to the Father, he humbled himself still more to become less than the rest of us— someone "from whom men hide their faces" (Is 53:3, RSV)— and he died on a cross.

Because of this act of love that so joined his humanity to his divine and eternal self-surrender as the Word of God, God the Father exalted him and gave to him the name—Yhwh. This is the very name of God himself, a word that is always translated in English as "Lord." Now, no one can "become" God or Lord, so this phrase must mean that Jesus in his human nature was ineffably transformed by the Father's act of raising him from the dead. The result is that we who "see" him by faith can now know who he is in the depth of his being: the Son of God, who merits the honor of the divine name, "Yhwh/ Lord."

The hymn goes on to say that at the name that Jesus now bears, "every knee should bow ... and every tongue confess." This is an allusion to one of the most monotheistic texts in the Bible. Yhwh is speaking:

> Turn to me and be saved, all the ends of the earth! For I am God, and there is no other. By myself I have sworn, from my mouth has gone forth in righteousness a word that shall not return: "To me every knee shall bow, every tongue shall swear." It shall be said of me "Only in Yhwh are righteousness and strength."
>
> ISAIAH 45:22-24, RSV

Since the Resurrection, every tongue must confess to the glory of God the Father, who freely bestowed the name, that *Jesus Christ* is Yhwh/Lord. Look at a crucifix, listen closely to the Passion narrative on this Sunday, and repeat in your heart, "Jesus Christ is Lord."

Monday of Holy Week
Isaiah 42:1-7; John 12:1-11

Chapter 40 of the Book of Isaiah begins a section that is known as "Second Isaiah." Interspersed in these chapters is the description of a just man, sometimes called the servant of Yhwh, whose role in the restoration of Israel is pivotal. He appears amid other oracles, and his countenance can hardly be made out, much like the figure of the suffering just man in the psalms. Yet, as will become apparent as we consider the four servant oracles, this man is a figure of someone to come, someone who will have many of the lineaments of Jeremiah but in and through whose sufferings the will of God will be given actual existence. The Church uses all four of these oracles or songs during Holy Week.

Today we have the first of the "Servant Songs." It is found in the opening verses of chapter forty-two of the Book of Isaiah. God, Yhwh, describes the one to come:

> Behold my servant, whom I uphold, my chosen, in whom my soul delights. I have put my Spirit upon him; he will bring forth justice to the nations. He will not cry or lift up his voice, or make it heard in the street; a bruised reed he will not break, and a dimly burning wick he will not quench; he will faithfully bring forth justice.
>
> ISAIAH 42:1-3, RSV

You may recognize here the words of the Father at Jesus' Baptism, the moment when Jesus openly embraced his vocation: "This is my Son, the beloved, in whom I take delight" (Mt 3:17).

In the Isaiah text God now directly addresses his servant:

> I am Yhwh, I have called you in righteousness, I have
> taken you by the hand and kept you; I have given you as
> a covenant to the people, a light to the nations, to open
> the eyes that are blind, to bring out the prisoners from
> the dungeon, from the prison those who sit in darkness.
>
> ISAIAH 42:6-7, RSV

This servant is a liberator whose work will bring freedom
and joy to the whole world.

The gospel tells us of a lavish gesture of love that provoked
the anger of a greedy man and was acknowledged by Jesus as
a preparation for his burial. As John narrates the incident (the
other Gospels have differing accounts), Mary, the sister of
Lazarus, takes a jar of extremely precious perfumed oil, worth
almost what a laborer would earn in a year, and pours it over
Jesus' feet. The fragrance of the perfume and the fragrance of
the gesture fill the house. Judas' question as expressed by
Mark is, "Why this waste?" (Mk 14:4). John tells us that Judas
was not even concerned for the poor but rather wished to get
his hands on the proceeds from the possible sale of the perfume.

Jesus first answers in defense of the woman, saying that this
anointing anticipates his burial. Mary, perhaps unknowingly, is
performing a prophetic gesture even as she honors Jesus and
shows him her love. Jesus then responds to Judas' false expression of concern for the "waste" of what could be given to the
poor by alluding to Deuteronomy 15:11, "For the poor will
never cease out of the land; therefore I command you, you
shall open wide your hand to your brother, to the needy and

to the poor, in the land." Judas is being told, "If your concern is for the poor, then take your own money and 'open wide your hand to your brother.'"

Our situation is different. First, in any genuine Christian community or parish there should never be great abundance on one hand and great need on the other. Luke portrays for us the life of the model community of Jerusalem by alluding to the same text in Deuteronomy: "There was not a needy person among them" (Acts 4:34, RSV).

The grace of Christ has changed what seemed to be a permanent condition in the Christian community. Now we can anoint the feet of Jesus both by pouring out our lives for him and by caring for his Body, the Church—especially the privileged members of that Body, the poor and needy right in our own midst. And the fragrance of our charity towards God and neighbor will fill the whole Church.

⚜

Tuesday of Holy Week
Isaiah 49:1-6; John 13:21-33, 36-38

In the reading from Isaiah we encounter the second Servant Song, and in the gospel we look upon the two betrayers of Jesus.

The servant first describes himself and his vocation. Like Jeremiah, he was called from his mother's womb (see Jer 1:5), and the Lord "made my mouth like a sharp sword, in the shadow of his hand he hid me; he made me a polished arrow, in his quiver he hid me away." Yet, like Jeremiah he knows suffering and failure as well as confidence in the plan of God: "I have

127

labored in vain, I have spent my strength for nothing and vanity; yet surely my right is with the Lord, and my recompense with my God." The Lord then promises him that his suffering will produce fruit: "I will give you as a light to the nations, that my salvation may reach to the end of the earth."

Jesus, the Servant in whom the vocation described above finds its fulfillment, also faces the thought that he has labored in vain. Yet he, too, knows that in him and in his obedient suffering the Father will be glorified. He first announces that, after all this time, one of his close friends is about to betray him. When Peter asks Jesus who it is, Jesus gives him a sign: "It is he to whom I shall give this morsel when I have dipped it." Then, "After Judas took the morsel, Satan entered him.... So, after receiving the morsel, he immediately went out; and it was night" (Jn 13:27-30).

At this moment Jesus bursts into prophecy: "Now is the Son of Man glorified, and in him God is glorified; if God is glorified in him, God will also glorify him in himself, and glorify him at once." God's plan of salvation for everyone, even Judas if somehow he accepts it, is now set firmly on its course.

Jesus further prophesies that he is about to leave his disciples, and this prompts Peter to protest, "Lord, why cannot I follow you now? I will lay down my life for you," only to receive this answer: "Will you lay down your life for me? Amen, amen, I say to you, the cock will not crow till you have denied me three times."

Here we see the other betrayer, and we realize that we are faced with a choice. Are we Judas or Peter? That we are betrayers is plain enough, is it not? We have made that choice often enough in our lives, but there is still another choice to be made. Will we take the guilt upon ourselves and despair like

Judas, or will we allow Jesus to look upon us as he did upon Peter? "And the Lord turned and looked at Peter. And Peter remembered the Word of the Lord, how he had said to him, 'Before the cock crows today, you will deny me three times.' And he went out and wept bitterly" (Lk 22:61-62, RSV).

In addition, therefore, to the theme of the suffering and triumph of the Servant, we are given today the opportunity to repent of our sins. Real repentance begins with a look from the Lord that gives us the courage to acknowledge what we have done. This is a work of the Holy Spirit, one for which we should earnestly pray, since we are only capable of discerning our sin in the light of the cross. As John Paul II tells us:

> The action of the Spirit of truth, which works toward salvific "convincing concerning sin," encounters in a person in this condition [of sin] an interior resistance, as it were an impenetrability of conscience, a state of mind which could be described as fixed by reason of a free choice. This is what Sacred Scripture usually calls "hardness of heart." ... Pope Pius XII had already declared that "the sin of the century is the loss of the sense of sin," and this loss goes hand in hand with the "loss of the sense of God."
>
> John Paul II
> *The Holy Spirit in the Life*
> *of the Church and the World,* 47

We should pray today not only for ourselves but for the whole world, that we may see our sin in the light of the cross of Christ. There we will see some of its true measure, and there we will see the love that beckons us to be reconciled to God and to receive forgiveness.

Wednesday of Holy Week
Isaiah 50:4-9; Matthew 26:14-25

On this day before the sacred *Triduum* (the three days of the Paschal Mystery), the Church, in the gospel, wants us to consider once again the sin of Judas and to hear the call of the Lord to repentance. Since contemplating the work of God on the cross does this most effectively, we will meditate today on the third and fourth Songs of the Servant, which are assigned to today and Good Friday respectively. There, as it were in the refracted light of prophecy, we will understand something of the greatness of what Jesus Christ has done for us.

In the third song, the prophetic mystic who has been given such an insight into God's plan lets the Servant speak again and describe the crucible in which salvation is brought about. It is a mystery of suffering and strength, of weakness and confidence in God. The Servant begins by describing his mission:

> The Lord, Yhwh, has given me a well-trained tongue so that I might console the weary with a word that stirs them. Morning by morning he opens my ear so that I might listen and learn. I have not rebelled nor turned back. I gave my back to those who beat me, my cheeks to those who tore my beard. I did not shield my face from blows and spittle.
>
> ISAIAH 50:4-6

The gospel writers were careful to allude to this prophecy when describing the mockery of Jesus at his trial: "And they all condemned him as deserving death. And some began to spit on him, and to cover his face, and to strike him, saying to him, 'Prophesy!' And the guards greeted him with blows" (Mk 14:64-65).

In the last of the songs the words of God himself both begin and end the people's message of astonishment and confession of sin. God begins:

> Behold, my servant shall succeed! He will be raised high, lifted up and exalted! Even as many were amazed at him: so marred beyond human his look, his visage beyond that of humankind. So shall he astonish many nations; because of him kings are speechless. For what was never told them they see, what they never heard they now ponder.
>
> Isaiah 52:13-15

We have once again in these words God's own description of his astonishing plan realized in the suffering and the glory of his Servant.

Next the people offer a lament over the Servant and over their own sins. It is here that we arrive at one of the highest points of the Israelite understanding of vicarious suffering. According to God's will, the Servant by his suffering is able to repair the broken covenant and bring the people back to God. This is a foreshadowing of the universal vocation of Jesus, the Servant who will bring the whole world back from its sin:

> Who would believe what we have heard? And the arm of Yhwh, to whom has it been revealed?... There was no form or comeliness that we should look at him, no beauty that we should desire him. Despised and forsaken by men, a man of sorrows and known by grief. As one from

whom men hide their faces, despised and we esteemed him not.

ISAIAH 53:1-3

Now the people express the truth of what they have seen:

Yet ours the grief that he carried, our sorrows and he bore them.... He was pierced for our rebellions, crushed for our sins. Upon him the discipline that makes us whole. By his stripes there is healing for us. All of us as sheep we wandered, each man turned his own way, and Yhwh caused to light upon him the guilt of us all.... He was given his grave with the wicked, with the corrupt his mound of repose. Though he had done no violence, nor was deceit on his lips.

ISAIAH 53:4-9

Finally, God takes up the word and vindicates his Servant in terms that foreshadow the Resurrection:

For the travail of his soul he shall see light, shall be sated. By his knowledge, the just one, my servant, shall justify many, and their sins he bears. Therefore I apportion him a share with the great, and with the mighty he shall share the spoil. Because he poured out his soul to death and was counted among the rebellious, yet he bore the sins of the many and for the wicked won favor.

ISAIAH 53:11-12

Gaze on Jesus now, and make this Servant Song personal to you: "Mine the grief that he carried, my sorrows and he bore them, he was pierced for my rebellions, crushed for my sins, by his stripes there is healing for me."

⚓

Holy Thursday: Evening Mass of the Lord's Supper
Exodus 12:1-8, 11-14; 1 Corinthians 11:23-26; John 13:1-15

The theme of Holy Thursday is the Eucharist, that of Good Friday is the Passion, Holy Saturday is a time of silent expectation, and Easter, beginning with the vigil, is the day of the Resurrection. We will meditate on each of these facets of the Paschal Mystery in turn, taking one each day.

Jesus gathered with his disciples to celebrate the rite of Passover. It is a memorial feast, commemorating God's deliverance of his people from slavery and his gift of freedom in the Promised Land. The lamb was slain, roasted, and eaten. Its blood was put on the doorpost to remind succeeding generations of the blood of the lamb that protected the Israelites from the angel who came to slay the firstborn in Egypt: "The blood shall be a sign for you, upon the houses where you are; and when I see the blood, I will pass over you, and no plague shall fall upon you to destroy you, when I smite the land of Egypt" (Ex 12:13, RSV).

Unleavened bread reminded the Israelites of the haste with which they left Egypt, and bitter herbs of the bitterness of their life of slavery. On that night Jesus carefully explained all these elements of the central feast of their people to his disciples. And in that light he explained the meaning of what was to take place in his own death and vindication.

The tradition of Jesus' actions that night was passed on and reenacted at his command. People gathered and repeated his gestures and words and knew his presence among them. In the second reading today Paul tells us explicitly: "I received from the Lord what I also delivered to you," referring most probably to his contact with Peter and the Jerusalem community some three to five years after Jesus' death and resurrection (see Gal 1:18). He then goes on to give us the liturgical account of Jesus' last supper as it was already celebrated, most likely in Antioch:

> Then the Lord Jesus on the night when he was betrayed took bread, and when he had given thanks, he broke it, and said, "This is my body which is for you. Do this in remembrance of me." In the same way also the cup, after supper, saying, "This cup is the new covenant in my blood. Do this, as often as you drink it, in remembrance of me."
>
> 1 CORINTHIANS 11:23-25, RSV

Ask the Holy Spirit to let you feel the intensity of love in those words. Jesus is giving himself to us in his Passion and in this Eucharist. "This is my body—my self—for you. Here, take this and eat it, make it a part of your very self, your own body. Be caught up in the act of love with which I die and rise, in which I now live. I give you my risen and glorious body. I give you myself because I love you. All other food you eat, you change into yourself; when you eat this bread, I change you into myself. I make you glorious. I prepare your body, your self, for an eternal and radiant existence. All of this because the body you eat is one that is given up to the Father in an immeasurable act of love."

Our Lord further tells us, "Do this in remembrance of me." "To remember," in the biblical phrase that Jesus uses, means to have his act of love in dying and giving himself so present to you that you are different. His act of love is the source of your living.

Then he took the cup and said, "This cup is the new covenant in my blood." At the first covenant, Moses took the blood of the animals and splashed it on the altar, which represented God, then he read the Book of the Covenant to the people. When they agreed to obey, he sprinkled them with the blood, thus binding them to God, and said: "This is the blood of the covenant, which the Lord has made with you" (Ex 24:6-8).

Many centuries later Jeremiah received a promise that God would one day provide a new covenant, and it would consist in this:

> I will put my law within them, and I will write it upon their hearts; and I will be their God, and they shall be my people. And no longer shall each man teach his neighbor and each his brother, saying, "Know the Lord," for they shall all know me, from the least of them to the greatest, says the Lord; for I will forgive their iniquity, and I will remember their sin no more.
>
> JEREMIAH 31:33-34, RSV

The blood of Jesus is the seal of this new covenant. We can know the Lord and know that our sins are forgiven by the act of love in which Jesus died for us. We share this by drinking his blood. That is why Paul concludes: "For as often as you eat this bread and drink the cup, you proclaim the Lord's death until he comes." Thank you, Lord Jesus.

Good Friday of the Lord's Passion
Isaiah 52:13–53:12; Hebrews 4:14-16; 5:7-9; John 18:1–19:42

Today our hearts concentrate on the Passion of the Lord. In the first reading we are introduced into Our Lord's vicarious suffering as it was prophesied in the fourth Servant Song, which we considered on Wednesday:

> Yet ours the grief that he carried, our sorrows and he bore them ... and he was pierced for our rebellions, crushed for our sins. Upon him the discipline that makes us whole. By his stripes there is healing for us. All of us as sheep we wandered, each man turned his own way, and Yhwh caused to light upon him the guilt of us all.
>
> ISAIAH 53:4-6

In the second reading we are brought into the inner sanctuary of Jesus' heart, where in a moment of decision he embraced the Father's will and gave his suffering an eternal meaning by his priestly offering:

> Who in the days of his flesh offered prayers and entreaties, with a strong cry and tears, to him who could save him from death, and he was heard because of his reverent submission. Though being Son, he learned obedience from what he suffered, and being made perfect, he became for all who obey him the source of eternal salvation being proclaimed by God high priest according to the order of Melchizedek.
>
> HEBREWS 5:7-10

In the gospel today we have the Passion narrative according to St. John. From this vast theological and mystical teaching on the Lord's suffering and death, we will consider only Jesus' dialogue with Pilate about truth. As you hear or read this Passion narrative, remember the words of the great theologian Origen. He said that no one can understand this gospel unless like John they have leaned on the breast of Jesus and taken Mary for their mother.

When the Jewish leaders bring Jesus to Pilate, they accuse him of being a criminal. When Pilate begins to question Jesus, he first asks if he is "the King of the Jews"—meaning, does he consider himself a rival to Caesar's authority in Palestine?

Jesus asks Pilate why he is asking the question and then responds to Pilate's further interrogation: "My kingdom is not from this world. If it were from this world, my subjects would be fighting that I not be handed over to the Jews; as it is, my kingdom is not from here."

Pilate pushes his question: "So you are a king."

Jesus responds, "You say I am a king," that is, the title is both apt and inept. He then delivers this solemn pronouncement concerning the nature of his mission and kingship: "For this I was born, and for this I came into the world, that I might bear witness to the truth. All those who are of the truth listen to my voice."

Pilate, frightened, asks the evasive question, "What is truth?" (Jn 18:33-38).

How do you answer Pilate? What does Jesus mean by identifying his kingdom with the truth and guaranteeing that all who listen to his voice are "of the truth"? The truth of which Jesus speaks is the truth of the cross. The fullness of the truth is the revelation of the Father; that is why Jesus can say of himself, "I am the way, the truth, and the life" (Jn 14:6, RSV). On the cross Jesus reveals the face of the Father: "God so loved the world that he gave his only begotten Son so that all who believe in him might not perish but might have eternal life. For God did not send his Son into the world that he might condemn the world, but that, through him, the world might be saved" (Jn 3:16-17).

The redeeming sacrifice of the cross reveals the truth, the true identity of the Father. Those who yield to this truth, who are thus "of the truth," recognize and listen to the voice of Jesus. He is their king because they have allowed his act of love on the cross to be the very life of their own life and actions. Together with their sisters and brothers they are the kingdom that is real enough in this world but which does not need the world to sustain it. In this sense Jesus' kingdom is not *of* this world, even though this world is being called to salvation by his voice.

The Church celebrates the kingdom of Christ by calling it "a kingdom of truth" (found in the Preface of Christ the King), while an ancient hymn for Good Friday sings of Christ, "God reigns from the wood of the cross" (*Vexilla Regis*). Jesus is most himself—he is most intensely the truth—in the act of love in which he gave himself to the Father for us. When we listen to his voice this self-revelation of the Son of God becomes within us "a fountain of water springing up to eternal life" (Jn 4:14).

Holy Saturday

There is no common gathering in the parish during this day, and apart from the Office of the day, there are no liturgical readings. It is a day of expectancy and silence. Expectancy, because in the darkness the cloud reveals the pillar of fire hidden within it and ready to burst into flame on Easter morning. Silence, because Jesus, in the tomb, is keeping the Sabbath as he prepares to begin a new creation. The following three passages capture some of the mood of this day. The first is taken from an ancient homily for Holy Saturday; the other two are modern poems.

An Ancient Homily

Something strange is happening—there is a great silence on earth today, a great silence and stillness. The whole earth keeps silence because the King is asleep. The earth trembled and is still because God has fallen asleep in the flesh, and he has raised up all who have slept since the world began. God has died in the flesh, and hell trembles with fear. He has gone to search for our first parent, as for a lost sheep.... He has gone to free from sorrow the captives Adam and Eve, he who is both God and the son of Eve. The Lord approached them bearing the cross, the weapon that had won him the victory. At the sight of him, Adam, the first man he had created, struck his breast in terror and cried out to everyone: "My Lord be with you all." Christ answered him: "And with your spirit." He took him by the hand and raised him up saying: "Awake, O sleeper, and rise from the dead, and Christ will give you light" (Eph 5:14)....

I slept on the cross, and a sword pierced my side for you who slept in paradise and brought forth Eve from your side. My side has healed the pain in yours. My sleep will rouse you from your sleep in hell. The sword that pierced me has sheathed the sword that was turned against you.

Rise, let us leave this place. The enemy led you out of the earthly paradise. I will not restore you to that paradise, but I will enthrone you in heaven. I forbade you the tree that was only a symbol of life, but see, I who am life itself am now one with you.... The bridal chamber is adorned, the banquet is ready, the eternal dwelling places are prepared, the treasure houses of all good things lie open. The kingdom of heaven has been prepared for you from all eternity.[1]

Adam

In the beginning
streams still mist
enfold me
as I sleep with red earth
awaiting light to tremble
and be born.

Life forms
on the breasts of shadows
rippling the dark
and reaching out
to stir the waters
moved by Wind-breath
on my heart.

True light
ungrasped by darkness
rises quickly from the tomb
whose wounded side
lies open
to desire
the pangs of childbirth
and see a man alive.

To quit the womb-life
of beginning
with arms outstretched
to touch the dawn
in setting stars
of life's blood
and the blinding light
of friend.

He who loses
his life
shall find it.

When I am thirsty,
give me to drink.
When I am dead
pour ointment on my body
and let the fragrance fill the sky
for love is stronger.[2]

In silence and rest is your salvation,
in quiet and trust your strength.

Within the tomb,
moon-shadows bow in time
to trees.
While the wind conjures
stars in harmonies
long forgotten.

What is restful as death,
or as silent?
The night
lowering on a tryst
where lovers' words once whispered
await some echo now.

Storm-pains beat
a raucous scar
upon the stone.
And yet no sound
is heard
within the grave
where only snow-flakes reach
and murmur out a mystery.

It is a candle flame
so strong that it invokes
the dawn fire
voice of song
and bursts the ground asunder.

Life colors leap
across his eyes,

and lie like garments
at his feet.
The quiet places music
on the breeze,
and turns the stone—
Christ is truly risen.[3]

The Easter Vigil

Readings: Genesis 1:1–2:2; Genesis 22:1-18; Exodus 14:15–15:1; Exodus 15:1-6, 17-18; Isaiah 54:5-14; Psalm 30:2, 4-6, 11-13; Isaiah 55:1-11; Isaiah 12:2-6; Baruch 3:9-15, 32–4:4; Psalm 19:8-11; Ezekiel 36:16-28; Psalm 42:3, 5; 43:3-4; Romans 6:3-11; Psalm 118:1-2, 16-17, 22-23; Matthew 28:1-10 (Cycle A); Mark 16:1-18 (Cycle B); Luke 24:1-12 (Cycle C)

From earliest times, in all the rites of the Church, the Easter Vigil has been characterized by a long period devoted to the Word of God. We listen to the Word and then respond with the Word in song. In the present Roman rite there are nine readings, seven from the Old Testament and two from the New. The first eight readings are always the same, while the last, the gospel, varies according to the cycle.

The Old Testament readings are meant to help us see the relation between the types of the Passion and the prophecies of a new era and a new covenant. These two realities, which became one at the cross and Resurrection, now coalesce in the mystery of the Sacraments of Initiation—Baptism, Confirmation, and the Eucharist—which are given to the catechumens at the Vigil.

We have come together with the catechumens throughout Lent; we have entered with them into the purifying action of the "scrutinies" as well as all the preparations of Lent. The first of the two New Testament readings this night is from St. Paul's Letter to the Romans (6:3-11) and is a treatise on the wonders of baptism. Since we will be called upon to renew the promises and rekindle the grace of our own baptism, let us meditate on the grace we will receive anew and the commitment that it entails.

Our passage begins, "Or are you unaware that we who were baptized into Christ Jesus were baptized into his death? So then, we were buried with him through baptism into death so that just as Christ was raised from the dead through the glory of the Father, so, too, we also might walk in newness of life." Baptism is an action of the most Holy Trinity in which the Father joins us to Christ, fixed in the act of love in which he died, and confers upon us the gift of the Holy Spirit so that we form one Body with Christ: "For by one Spirit we were all baptized into one body—Jews or Greeks, slaves or free—and all were made to drink of one Spirit" (1 Cor 12:13, RSV).

Being baptized into the death of Christ means having Christ dwell in us, now glorious and raised "through the glory of the Father." In his power we are able to die to sin. The word *sin* refers not primarily to our individual acts of sin but to the whole regime of sin, that complex of human rebellion and inhumanity that finds expression in the structures of the whole mode of life that characterizes "the world." When we die to sin, we are free of the power of that complex of social, political, cultural, economic, psychological, and spiritual forces that rule this world.

Our individual acts of sin are the ways in which we connive

in and yield to these forces. We appropriate sin and make it our own. Paul tells us that we are free from this power if we consent to the new power at work in us. Jesus Christ, by his love and obedience in death, died to the forces that make up sin in this world. Because he lives in us, we, too, have been transferred to a new realm of existence. We can experience this, not as a theory but as an actual fact, if we call upon that power when we are faced with those memories and habits of sin that keep us slaves to sin. This is how Paul expresses it:

> Knowing this: our old man [the self we once were] was co-crucified so that the body of sin [our past habits of connivance] might be rendered impotent, in order that we no longer be slaves to sin.... If then we died with Christ, we believe that we will live with him; knowing that Christ, raised from the dead, will die no more; death has power over him no longer. The death he died he died to sin, once for all; the life he lives he lives to God. So, too, you count yourselves dead to sin but living to God in Christ Jesus.
>
> ROMANS 6:6-11

Jesus lives to God the Father, and we, in the depths of our spirit, have been given a share in this life achieved through death. His death has set us free from needing to capitulate to sin or even to our past habits of capitulation. This can be a matter of experience for you if you will consciously, in faith, repent for your sins, turn to Jesus Christ, and let the power of his cross give you authority over your own life. It is because of this new and risen life that the Paschal Mystery is Good News.

❧
Easter Sunday

Acts 10:34, 37-43; Colossians 3:1-4; John 20:1-9

The readings on Easter Sunday are a model of simplicity and depth. In the first reading we have a summary of Peter's speech in the house of Cornelius. Listen to the clarity with which the basic gospel message is preached:

> God anointed Jesus with the Holy Spirit and power; he went about doing good and healing all those who had been overpowered by the devil because God was with him. And we are witnesses of all that he did both in the territory of the Jews and in Jerusalem. Him they killed, hanging him on wood: this man God raised up on the third day and granted that he be made manifest not to all the people but to witnesses chosen beforehand by God.... And he commanded us to announce to the people and to bear witness that he is the one designated by God [as] judge of the living and the dead. To him all the prophets witness that all who believe in him receive forgiveness of sins through his name.
>
> Acts 10:38-43

The result of Peter's speech was that "as Peter was still speaking these things, the Holy Spirit fell on all those hearing the word."

Today, recite the Creed slowly, or pray the glorious mysteries of the rosary, and let the greatness of what we proclaim come alive to you. Pray that the Holy Spirit come down upon you and your family as he did through Peter's words on the house of Cornelius.

The message of the second reading, from the Letter to the

Colossians, is very similar to that from the Letter to the Romans, chapter six, which we reflected upon last night. The Gospel of John, however, opens up another dimension of the mystery of the Resurrection: that of an encounter with the living Christ. In fact, chapter twenty of the Gospel of John contains the narrative of four encounters.

The first encounter is with the beloved disciple; it is an encounter of "absence." This encounter is in the text for today (see Jn 20:1-9). The encounter takes place because the beloved disciple "saw" the cloths that were on the dead body of Jesus and "began to believe." He allowed the evidence of the cloths and that of Jesus' absence to lead him to a complete understanding of what had happened: "And then the other disciple also went in, the one who came first to the tomb, and he saw and began to believe. [He could go no further in his belief.] For they did not yet know the scripture, that he had to rise from the dead" (Jn 20:8-9).

The second encounter is with Mary Magdalene after the disciples "went off again to their homes." There is initial misunderstanding, but then Jesus takes the initiative and calls Mary by her name. Here is an encounter of presence and recognition:

Jesus said to her, "Mary." Turning, she said to him (in Hebrew), "Rabbuni" (which means "Teacher"). Jesus said to her, "Stop clinging to me, for I have not yet ascended to the Father. Go, rather, to my brothers and say to them, I ascend to my Father and your Father, to my God and your God." Mary the Magdalene went, announcing to the disciples, "I have seen the Lord!"

JOHN 20:16-18

Mary becomes the apostle to the apostles, and her proclamation, based on her encounter with the presence of Jesus, is a mature act of faith. She does not say, "I have seen Jesus," but, "I have seen *the Lord.*"

The third encounter is with the apostles themselves. Jesus comes to them, locked in their hideaway, greets them with "Peace," and then confers the Holy Spirit on them and gives them a mission to the whole world. Already we see the fulfillment of the promise made to the disciples of all time: "I will not leave you orphans, I am coming to you. Yet a little while and the world will see me no longer; but you will see me, because I live, and you too will live. On that day you will know that I am in my Father, and you in me, and I in you" (Jn 14:18-20). The result is that the disciples are able to tell Thomas, who was absent, "We have seen the Lord." Thomas demands that he put Jesus to the test before he will accept the witness of the others.

This leads to the fourth and final encounter, when Jesus comes once again and challenges Thomas. "Thomas answered and said to him, 'My Lord and my God!' Jesus said to him, 'Because you have seen me, you have believed; blessed are those who have not seen and have believed'" (Jn 20:28-29). The paradox is clear: those who believe without seeing begin to see. "You will see me, because I live, and you, too, will live."

Herein consists our invitation to accept the proclamation of the Church and grow in faith, coming to know Jesus more intimately until we, too, have an encounter with the living Lord. Here are two descriptions, by Pope John Paul II, of this encounter: "This intense life of prayer must be adapted to the capacity and condition of each Christian, so that in all the different situations of life each one may be able 'to drink of the one Spirit' (cf. 1 Cor 12:13) from the wellspring of their encounter with Christ." And again, "The Eucharist is the outstanding moment of encounter with the living Christ" (*The Church in America* #29, 33). Let this, then, be our final word on the feast of Easter.

CHAPTER EIGHT

The Sundays of Lent, Cycle B
The Power of Baptism

So that all the faithful can hear as much of Sacred Scripture as possible, the Church has established three different cycles for the Sunday readings and two cycles for the daily readings. The three Sunday cycles are maintained for Lent, while the cycles for the daily readings are not maintained for Lent or Advent. In this chapter, then, we will meditate on the readings in the second cycle, called cycle B, while in the next chapter we will meditate on the readings for cycle C.

❧

The First Sunday of Lent, Cycle B
Genesis 9:8-15; 1 Peter 3:18-22; Mark 1:12-15

In all three cycles the gospel for the first Sunday of Lent narrates the temptation of Jesus while the first two readings present some specific theme. This year the theme is Baptism, since one of the key aspects of Lent is the preparation of the catechumens for the Sacraments of Initiation, whose foundation is Baptism. As the *Catechism of the Catholic Church* (1213) says: "Holy Baptism is the basis of the whole Christian life, the gateway to life in the Spirit, and the door which gives access to the other sacraments."

The reading in Genesis tells us about the covenant God made with Noah after the flood. He promised, "The waters shall never again become a flood to destroy all flesh," and he used the rainbow as a sign of the solidity of this promise (Gn 9:15, RSV).

The First Letter of Peter takes up the story of Noah and states that Baptism is the "antitype" of the waters through which Noah and his family were brought to safety. In Greek, a "type" is most often something that has received an impression or shape from something else. The ancients sealed documents by impressing the seal from their ring (the "antitype") upon wax, which then bore the imprint (the "type") of the original. St. Peter is telling us that, in some mysterious fashion, baptism impressed its "shape" upon the incident that preceded it: namely the preservation of Noah during the time of the flood. The reality of Christ and his saving activity is thus the "model" and source for the events mediated to us by the Old Testament.

We should first note that the discussion of Baptism is introduced by pointing to the source of its power—namely, the death and resurrection of Jesus Christ: "For Christ has suffered once and for all for sin, the Just for the unjust, in order to lead you to God, being put to death in the flesh, but made alive in the Spirit" (1 Pt 3:18). Jesus, our Lord, the "antitype," the one whose stamp is borne by the Servant in the prophecies of Isaiah (which we read in Holy Week), has suffered for us and freed us from our sins. Now that he has been "made alive in the Spirit," he can communicate the saving power of his death to us. This is the significance of Baptism, which is called the "sacrament of faith."

The letter first speaks of the initial beneficiaries of Jesus' death in his human nature, his "flesh." A mysterious passage tells us how Jesus, after his death, went to those who were being held captive in death and freed them: "He went and preached to the spirits in prison, who once had been disobedient, as God's patience waited in the days of Noah as the ark was being built, in which a few, namely eight souls, were delivered through the water" (1 Pt 3:19-20). "Jesus, like all men, experienced death, and in his soul he joined the others in the realm of the dead. But he descended there as Savior, proclaiming the Good News to the spirits imprisoned there" (*Catholic Catechism*, 632). Reflect on the humility of Jesus, the Son of God, who, as we state in the Apostles' Creed, *"descended to the dead."* Is there any depth to which he will not go in order to bring you to life?

St. Peter next shows us how this same liberating power of Jesus reaches us:

Baptism, as an antitype of this [that is, Jesus' freeing of the spirits in prison and all that it implies] now delivers you—not as the putting away of dirt from the flesh but as the entreaty to God for a good conscience—through the resurrection of Jesus Christ, who is at the right hand of God after having gone into heaven while the angels, authorities, and powers were made subject to him.

1 PETER 3:21-22

In brief, Baptism delivers us through the resurrection of Jesus Christ, who is now at the right hand of the Father. Baptism is an objective work of God (more real than the deliverance of Noah and his family) by which we are transferred into the kingdom of his beloved Son. Therefore, Baptism is not a mere ceremony; it is a sacrament that draws its power from Jesus, who is now glorious in the act of love in which he died. Seen from our side, God's action is an "entreaty to God for a good conscience." From God's side, it is the conferral of the source of that good conscience, namely, a share in the very life of Christ.

The Church gives us this season of Lent so that what was prophesied in the Old Testament and fulfilled in the New may be a living reality in our daily lives. We can know for ourselves freedom from all that leads to spiritual death.

⚜

The Second Sunday of Lent, Cycle B
Genesis 22:1-2, 9-13, 15-18; Romans 8:31-34; Mark 9:2-10

In all three cycles the Second Sunday of Lent is dedicated to a consideration of Abraham and to the mystery of the Transfiguration. In cycle B Paul presents Abraham in the second reading as a prefiguration, a "type," of God the Father himself, who "did not spare his own Son" (Rom 8:32, RSV). At the same time, Abraham's faith, trust, and obedience can help us get a glimpse into the heart of Jesus and learn from him how to live our own Christian lives. Then, in the gospel account of the Transfiguration, we hear the Father's voice declare that Jesus is his "beloved Son."

The Genesis text opens with telling us what is going to take place even though Abraham does not know it: "God put Abraham to the test." God calls his name and Abraham answers, "Here I am." In Hebrew this phrase indicates a com-

154

plete openness to hear and carry out what is going to follow. Rashi, a great medieval Jewish commentator, said of this response that it is characteristic of a just man that he is willing to carry out God's will even before he knows what it is.

God gives his command: "Take your son, your only son, Isaac, whom you love, and go to the land of Moriah. There you shall offer him as a holocaust on one of the mountains I will indicate to you." The drama of the text continues immediately: "And Abraham got up early in the morning and saddled his donkey, and he took two men with him and Isaac his son, and he split the sacrifice wood, and he arose and went toward the place which God indicated to him" (Gn 22:2-4).

God had promised Abraham, "I will make of you a great nation, and I will bless you, and make your name great, so that you will be a blessing." And he further specified, "Your own son shall be your heir" (Gn 12:2; 15:4). Isaac was Abraham's only son by Sarah, his beloved wife, and Isaac was the living concrete proof of the authenticity of God's promise. Yet now Abraham is told to sacrifice this beloved son and deprive himself of the only indication he has of God's fidelity to his promises.

> By faith Abraham, when he was tested, offered up Isaac, and he who had received the promises was ready to offer up his only son, of whom it was said, "Through Isaac shall your descendants be named." He considered that God was able to raise men even from the dead; hence, as a foreshadowing, he received him back.
>
> HEBREWS 11:17-19, RSV

This is Abraham, our father in faith. He believed God, and when put to the test, he trusted that God would be faithful to his promises. He was willing to sacrifice Isaac, the light of his life and the only tangible evidence he had that God was acting on his promise. In this he was also both the father and the type of Jesus, who as his son and Lord also trusted the Father right through death: "Son though he was he learned obedience from what he suffered; and being made perfect, he became for all who obey him the source of eternal salvation" (Heb 5:8-9).

However, the most remarkable allusion to the sacrifice of Abraham is found in the second reading, where we find Paul's description of the Father, who "did not spare his own Son, but handed him over for us all" (Rom 8:32). The notion that the Father is the source of Jesus' mission to death is found frequently in the New Testament: "In this God's love appeared among us: God has sent his Son, his Only Begotten, into the world that we might live through him. In this is the love: not that we have loved God, but that he loved us and sent his Son as an offering to deal with our sins" (1 Jn 4:9-10).

This theme is continued when we hear that the Father "handed over" Jesus for us all. No one reading the New Testament can fail to catch the allusion to the events of the Passion designated by this phrase. Judas "hands over" Jesus to the Jews, who "hand him over" to Pilate, who "hands him over" to death. Why would Paul use this phrase of the Father?

St. Thomas Aquinas, in his commentary on this verse, ponders the same question. This is his answer: "God the Father handed him over to death, first by decreeing that he become incarnate and suffer, and then by inspiring his human will with such a powerful love that he enthusiastically underwent his passion." Pray that you, too, will be invited into this dialogue of love between the Father and the Son.

The Third Sunday of Lent, Cycle B
Exodus 20:1-17; 1 Corinthians 1:22-25; John 2:13-25

An attentive reading of some lines in today's passage from the Book of Exodus can reveal the central theme of this Sunday. This theme is precisely that neither signs nor wisdom can bring us to faith, but rather only the love of God that is manifest in the death and resurrection of Jesus Christ. We should notice first of all how the Lord identifies himself as Savior: "I, Yhwh, am your God, who brought you out of the land of Egypt, from the house of slavery" (Ex 20:2). The obedience we give to God springs from our gratitude for what he has already done for us. We, all of us, were held in the thralldom of sin and death. He has freed us from this slavery, freed us to serve him.

It is only after revealing what he has done for us that God speaks his words of command. To worship him alone, never to make counterfeit gods that are more comfortable, to respect his reality and his name, and to set aside time to cease from our striving and give ourselves in trust to him—these are the ways to live out our relationship with him. Then, to honor our parents, have respect for life, be faithful to our spouse, respect the property and name of our neighbor—these guarantee that we will live in fidelity to the humanity he has given us.

The grateful heart continues to search for an ever deeper understanding of the mind of the Father and an ever more profound gratitude to him. We see this, for example, when Jesus tells us that not only adultery but also lustful looks are a means of using someone and offending his or her dignity. Or again, when he tells us that not only murder can deprive of life; also all words of injury and insult can take away the esteem and respect that are due human life (see Mt 5:17-48). Those who know what God has done for them seek earnestly to please the Father by learning from him how to live as human beings, as his children.

St. Paul, in his First Letter to the Corinthians, points us in the same direction: "Jews demand signs and Greeks seek wisdom, but we preach Christ crucified, a stumbling block to Jews and folly to Gentiles, but to those who are called, both Jews and Greeks, Christ is the power of God and the wisdom of God" (1 Cor 1:22-24, RSV). Once again we see that the response God wants is not admiration of his power or more apparent manifestations of wisdom, but rather an appreciation of what he has done for us and an acceptance of the gift of life he has given us in Christ crucified. There we can see, in fact, that "the foolishness of God is wiser than human wisdom, and the weakness of God is stronger than human strength" (1 Cor 1:25). The glorious cross of Christ is the very sign that confounds sensation seekers, and it is the very wisdom that offends those who look for the delight that the world has to offer.

The theme of seeking to enter more deeply into the will of the Father out of gratitude and the theme of understanding the wisdom and power of God manifest in the cross meet in the gospel. There we read how Jesus cleansed his Father's house of those who would turn it into a place of commerce. They may have thought themselves observant of the law, but they had forgotten the reason for the temple and lacked a sense of grateful prayer for all that God had done for them. Jesus understood the inner meaning of his Father's will and told them: "Take these things away; you shall not make my Father's house a marketplace" (Jn 2:16).

When he was challenged to produce some show of power, or some sign to legitimate his action, Jesus responded: "Destroy this temple, and in three days I will raise it up" (Jn 2:19, RSV). The sign is precisely the destruction and raising up of his body. It is a sign manifesting both "the weakness of God" and the "folly of God." For those who can see, however, it is the manifestation of a love whose only response is to receive the gift in faith and make a return of love. Look on this sign, and let the Holy Spirit teach you to praise God for the glorious cross of Christ.

꽃

The Fourth Sunday of Lent, Cycle B
2 Chronicles 36:14-16, 19-23;
Ephesians 2:4-10; John 3:14-21

One of the most prominent themes to be found in the readings of today is that of conversion. Clearly the Church has in mind those who are preparing for Baptism, but perhaps in a deeper way these readings are directed to us, the believers who are meant to reflect on sin and the mercy of God. In the passage we have today from the Letter to the Ephesians, we can see most clearly the rhythm of conversion from sin and darkness to the freedom and light of God. We will reflect on this text.

The first three verses of Ephesians chapter 2 (which are not in our reading) describe the situation from which we have come. Some Christians can see in these verses a description of what their lives once actually were. All Christians know that the external appearance of their lives might not have corresponded to this description, but that their hearts corresponded to what is said here:

> And you, being dead in your transgressions and your sins in which you once walked, according to the age of this world,... of the spirit now working in the sons of disobedience, among whom we ourselves once lived our life in the desires of our flesh, carrying out the desires of the flesh and of our inner impulses, and we were by nature children of wrath just like the rest.
>
> EPHESIANS 2:1-3

The reason for looking at where we were, or could have been, is to maintain in our hearts a deep sense of gratitude for the work that God has done in Christ and has communicated to us through faith and Baptism:

> But God, being rich in mercy, because of his great love with which he loved us, when we ourselves were dead in our transgressions, brought us to life with Christ—by grace you are saved—and raised us up with him, and seated us with him in the heavenly realm in Christ Jesus, so that he might demonstrate in the ages to come the surpassing wealth of his grace in his kindness toward us in Christ Jesus.
>
> EPHESIANS 2:4-7

Our author here uses one of his favorite phrases: God is "rich in mercy." He then goes on to describe the eternal life that is already ours, even in this life. We have been brought to life with Christ; we are seated with him in the heavenly realm.

It is reported that once God the Father said to St. Catherine of Siena that if she were to see the true glory of a person in the state of grace, she would be tempted to fall down and worship, so great is that glory. Already, then, the angels can see what we all will see one day, and then "the ages to come" will appreciate "the surpassing wealth of his grace—his kindness to us in Christ Jesus."

The passage concludes with another mention of God's gift of salvation to us and then goes on to speak of the personal mission he has confided to each one of us: "By grace you are saved, through faith; and this not from yourselves: the gift is of God. Not from works, so that no one may boast. For we are his handiwork, created in Christ Jesus for good works which God prepared beforehand so that we might walk by them" (Eph 2:8-10).

The "place" where these good works were prepared is twofold: heaven and the Church. Before the foundation of the world we were chosen in Christ to be "holy and blameless in his sight, in love" (Eph 1:4). This plan of God touches our lives when "by grace we are saved, through faith," and baptized into the Church, for there is but "one Lord, one faith, one baptism" (Eph 4:6). The works prepared for us are dwelling within us—with the Holy Spirit, who is moving us into conformity with Christ.

The full fruit of our conversion, then, is a life that gives glory to God and hope to the people who see us. Our lives are meant to witness to this power at work in us, making our lives genuinely human and our families places of peace and compassion. Our Lord already told us this: "Let your light so shine before men, that they may see your good works and give glory to your Father who is in heaven" (Mt 5:16, RSV). This is our privilege and our prayer.

The Fifth Sunday of Lent, Cycle B
Jeremiah 31:31-34; Hebrews 5:7-9; John 12:20-33

The prophecy of Jeremiah found in our first reading is one of the most important passages in the Old Testament. In fact, it is the longest quote from the Old Testament to be found in the New (Heb 8:8-12). The Church places the text here in order to show us that the fruit of Our Lord's passion and resurrection is a genuine interior change in those who accept it. The promise is that God will place within us the dynamic principle by which we can respond to him, while acknowledging his authority and coming to an intimate knowledge of him: "I will place my law within them and write it upon their hearts.... All from the least to the greatest will know me, for I will forgive their wrongdoing, and their sin I will remember no more" (Jer 31:33-34).

The mystery of Jesus' own interior struggle just before his Passion—located at Gethsemane in the Gospels of Matthew, Mark, and Luke—is alluded to in the passage from the Letter to the Hebrews and figures largely in the gospel text from John. Hebrews portrays Jesus as the suffering just man "who, in the days of his flesh, offered prayers and entreaties to him who could save him from death with a strong cry and tears. He was heard because of his reverent submission, and Son though he was, he learned obedience from what he suffered" (Heb 5:7-8). Now that he has been made perfect—that is, made a priest and transformed in his humanity so as to be apt for heavenly life—he is the source of eternal salvation for all who obey him.

The passage from John 12 contains several incidents situated here by the author just as Jesus' public life is closing. The first incidents mark a turning point. Some Greeks, who have come up to worship at the Feast of the Passover, approach Philip and say to him, "Sir, we want to see Jesus." When this is reported to Jesus, he recognizes that the moment has arrived to begin that process whose final result will be the gathering of all God's children together: "The hour has come that the Son of Man be glorified. Amen, amen, I say to you: unless the grain of wheat, falling into the ground, die, it remains alone; but if it die, it bears much fruit." Jesus foresees the fruit of his own "falling into the ground," and he knows that the hour has come for his glorification, which is precisely his being lifted up on the cross and exalted from the cross.

Then the moment of decision already spoken of in the Letter to the Hebrews as Christ's "reverent submission" is portrayed here.

> "Now my soul is troubled; and what should I say? Father, save me from this hour?—But for this have I come to this hour. Father, glorify your name!"
>
> A voice from heaven came: "I glorified it and I will glorify it again."
>
> The crowd, standing and listening, said there had been thunder; others said: an angel has spoken to him. Jesus answered and said: "Not for me did the voice come, but for you."
>
> JOHN 12:27-30

Jesus says that his soul is troubled, in words reminiscent of the report in the other Gospels: "My soul is sorrowful, enough to die; wait here and be on the watch." Jesus prays and submits himself to the will of the Father: "Abba, Father, all things are possible to you; take this cup away from me; but not what I will but what you will" (Mk 14:34-36). Here we see this same rhythm of prayer and submission: "And what should I say? Father, save me from this hour?—But for this have I come to this hour. Father, glorify your name!"

This is the beginning and the source of the new covenant: "I will place my law within them and write it upon their hearts." This deep inner submission with love and trust in the heart of Jesus prepares a similar place in our own hearts if we yield to it.

The concluding lines of our passage show us the fruit of Jesus' passion: "'Now is the judgment of this world, now the prince of this world will be cast out; and I, if I be lifted up from the earth, will draw all to myself.' He said this signifying by what kind of death he was going to die" (Jn 12:31-33). The prince of this world has been cast out of this world, and Jesus, now glorified and exalted on the cross, is able to draw all men and women, indeed the whole universe, to himself. "We adore you, O Christ, and we bless you, because by your holy cross you have redeemed the world."

⚜

Palm Sunday of the Lord's Passion, Cycle B
The Passion According to Mark, Mark 14:1-15:47

Only the two gospel passages of this day vary from cycle to cycle; the other readings are the same as those of cycle A. Leaving aside a consideration of Mark's account of the entry into Jerusalem, we will concentrate on the events that took place at Golgotha as they are narrated in the second gospel's Passion narrative.

Mark's restrained account allows us nevertheless to see some of the inner suffering of Jesus as well as the physical suffering. We should first observe how alone Jesus is. His disciples have left him, his choice for a leader has just denied him, the soldiers have beaten him and mocked him, and now:

> When the soldiers had made sport of him, they took the purple off him and put his own clothes on him; and they led him out to crucify him. And they pressed into service a certain man passing by, Simon the Cyrenian, who was coming in from the field, the father of Alexander and Rufus, so that he should carry his cross.
>
> MARK 15:20-21

They led him out to crucify him. The man to be crucified was made to carry the crossbeam of his cross—the upright beam was permanently in place at the execution site—and to bear a placard around his neck with the charge against him written on it. Jesus' placard said something like "King of the Jews."

Even at this early stage we are drawn into the action—reading the Passion is not a spectator activity. Because Jesus had been so weakened by the beating he took with whips, he needed help in carrying the crossbeam. Simon, a man from North Africa (Cyrene) whose sons were known to Mark's community in Rome, was pressed into service. Mark is careful to point out that this was "so that he should carry his [Jesus' and his own] cross." We are to think of Jesus' words: "If anyone wants to come after me, let him deny himself, and take up his cross, and continually follow me" (Mk 8:34). While Simon was pressed into service, we have entered this service of our own accord.

"And they brought him to the place called Golgotha, that is, translated, Skull Place. And they tried to give him wine drugged with myrrh, but he did not take it. And they crucified him; and they divided his clothes, throwing lots for them, who would take what" (Mk 15:22-24).

All Roman executions took place near a city gate so that those entering and leaving would see and be frightened. Golgotha, Skull Place, was probably a hillock just outside the wall of old Jerusalem, near a gate whose remains can be seen in the basement of the convent of the Orthodox nuns near the Church of the Holy Sepulchre.

The victim was usually stripped, but because of Jewish sensibilities this may have been modified. It was a pious Jewish custom to offer a man about to be crucified a drink of wine and myrrh to dull the pain. The custom was based on a line in the Book of Proverbs (31:6): "Give strong drink to a man about to perish, wine for the heart that is full of bitterness: let him drink and forget his misfortune, and remember his misery no more." Jesus refused the offer, preferring to know all the pain that his Father willed for him and thus to express his love.

"And they crucified him." No one in the ancient world needed any more details. It would be equivalent to saying today, "And they electrocuted him." Even Romans recognized the horror of the punishment; they called it a most wretched death and exempted Roman citizens from such a form of execution. Nails were driven into the wrists, and the man was affixed to the crossbeam, which was then hoisted onto the upright piece so that the victim was about two or three feet off the ground. Then his feet were nailed. Death usually came by asphyxiation when the weight of the body closed the diaphragm. Breaking the victim's legs assured a swift death, since the crucified man would no longer be able to support his weight.

And when it was the sixth hour darkness came on the whole land until the ninth hour. And at the ninth hour, Jesus cried out with a loud voice: "Eli, Eli, lamma sabacthani?" That is, translated, "My God, my God, why have you abandoned me?" ... But Jesus, letting out a loud cry, breathed out his last. And the curtain of the temple was torn in two from the top to the bottom. The centurion, who was standing by, opposite him, seeing that he breathed out his last in such a way, said: "Truly, this man was the Son of God."

MARK 15:33-39

Jesus is completely alone, yet he expresses this loneliness with the opening words of a psalm (Psalm 22) whose second part is a celebration of God's deliverance of the poor man. Finally he gives a loud cry and dies. The pagan soldier standing there has eyes to see and ears to hear. The first fruits of the pagan world, he makes his confession of faith: Jesus is the Son of God.

Stand there now, before the cross, and see the love of God for you, and recognize who it is who has died to give you life. Make your own confession of faith in Jesus, the Son of God.

The Easter Vigil Gospel, Cycle B
Mark 16:1-7

As soon as the sun had set, thus ending the Sabbath, the day after Jesus died, three women went and procured spices in order to anoint Jesus' body. They waited to go to the tomb until the first rays of dawn on the "first day of the week," the day after the Sabbath.

> When the Sabbath was passed, Mary the Magdalene, and Mary the mother of James, and Salome bought spices, so that they could go anoint him. And very early on the first day of the week, they came to the tomb, the sun having risen. And they were saying to each other: "Who will roll back the stone for us from the door of the tomb?" And looking up they saw that the stone had been rolled back; it was very large.
>
> MARK 16:1-4

It is important to realize that the early Christians were not frantically studying the pages of the Gospels, even after they were written, in order to find out if Jesus were risen from the dead. They *knew* he was risen because they experienced him in their midst; they were aware of his healing power and rejoiced to praise the Father in and through him. The gospel accounts of the Resurrection, while they are reporting events, are telling them in a way that allows us to understand the inner meaning of this mystery whose existence was taken for granted by those who first experienced it.

The women thus arrive at the tomb only to find the large

circular stone, which would have been rolled upright across the mouth of the tomb, already rolled back. "And going into the tomb, they saw a young man sitting on the right, clothed in a white robe; and they were awestruck. And he said to them: Do not be afraid; you are seeking Jesus, the Nazarene, the one crucified. He has been raised; he is not here. See the place where they laid him" (Mk 16:5-6).

Here is the basic Easter proclamation: The Crucified One is alive. Jesus, the Nazarene, is still "the one crucified." He has not rejected anything of his life among us. That is why his life, now transformed by the Resurrection, is the source of our life. Now we can begin to be disciples. This is the message the women are to deliver to *Peter* (the one who denied him!) and the others.

"But go, tell his disciples and Peter: He goes ahead of you to Galilee; there you will see him as he told you" (Mk 16:7). Jesus, even as he prophesied Peter's denials, told the disciples in effect that they would meet once again in Galilee, where they had first begun their discipleship. Jesus had said to them, "You will all fall away; for it is written, 'I will strike the shepherd, and the sheep will be scattered.' But after I am raised up, I will go before you to Galilee" (Mk 14:27-28).

All of us are invited to Galilee to begin again, to accept our vocation as disciples. We learn from the risen Jesus as he builds his Church, sending us to announce the Good News and guiding us to eternal glory.

CHAPTER NINE

The Sundays of Lent, Cycle C Strength for the Journey

The First Sunday of Lent, Cycle C

Deuteronomy 26:4-10; Romans 10:8-13; Luke 4:1-13

Once again, on this first Sunday of Lent we have an account of Jesus' temptation in the wilderness, this time from St. Luke's Gospel. It is preceded by an ancient credo of Israel and St. Paul's teaching on the accessibility of faith and its absolute importance. Because the theme of the temptation in the wilderness is so important to the Church during Lent, our meditation will concentrate there with the help of Fyodor Dostoyevsky.

In his epic novel *The Brothers Karamasov*, Dostoyevsky has a long passage in which Aloyosha comes to visit his older brother Ivan. Ivan tells Aloyosha that he plans to write a poem about "the Grand Inquisitor" and proceeds to describe it to him. The setting is Seville, in the sixteenth century. Jesus comes to visit his people; some recognize him and call out to him for help and healing, and he responds. Then, on the steps of the cathedral, Jesus encounters the bier of a young girl of seven who is being carried out for burial. The crowd begs him to raise her, and he does so. Watching from the other side of the street is the Cardinal, Grand Inquisitor, a tall ascetic man of ninety years who finally orders Jesus' arrest.

Later in the night, all alone, the Grand Inquisitor visits Jesus in his cell and begins to question him; Jesus remains silent. In effect, the Inquisitor says: "Why are you here? Why have you come back? You came and offered men freedom, and that was your mistake. Humans do not want to be free; they want to be safe. It has taken us nearly fifteen hundred years to undo your mistake.

"*The terrible and wise spirit, the spirit of self-destruction and nonexistence, the great spirit talked with you and we are told in the books that he apparently 'tempted' you.*[1] You could have changed those stones into bread, and men would have followed you and hung onto your every word, but you preferred to leave them free. We on the other hand know what they need. We have deceived them, and they willingly let themselves be deceived for the sake of the bread we give them.

"*They will marvel at us and they will regard us as gods because, having become their masters, we consented to endure freedom and rule over them—so dreadful will freedom become to them in the end! But we shall tell them that we do your bidding and rule in your name. We shall deceive them again, for we shall not let you come near us again. That deception will be our suffering, for we shall be forced to lie. That was the meaning of the first question in the wilderness, and that was what you rejected in the name of freedom, which you put above everything else.*

"The first temptation dealt with miracle, the second with mystery. You could have thrown yourself off the parapet of the temple and forced the angels to catch you. *Oh, you understood perfectly then that in taking one step, in making a move to cast yourself down, you would at once have tempted God and have lost all your faith in him, and you would have been dashed to pieces against the earth you came to save, and the wise spirit that tempted you would have rejoiced.... You did not come down from the cross when they shouted to you, mocking and deriding you.*

"They challenged you, but you still preferred a love that was free to obedience coerced. This once again was your mistake. Men will willingly trade the burden of their freedom for the comfort of being told what to do and the pleasure of fearing and hating those who command them.

"We have corrected your great work and have based it on miracle, mystery and authority. And men rejoiced that they were once more led like sheep and that the terrible gift which had brought them so much suffering had at last been lifted from their hearts. You could have taken over all the power, the authority of this world when that spirit showed you the kingdoms and rulers of the world. But you rebuked him, and that power crucified you.

"Why did you reject that last gift? By accepting the last counsel of the mighty spirit, you would have accomplished all that man seeks on earth, that is to say, whom to worship (the source of miracle), *to whom to entrust his conscience* (the possessor of mystery), *and how at last to unite all in a common, harmonious, and incontestable ant-hill, for the need of universal unity is the third and last torment of men."* Finished, the Inquisitor opens the cell door, and Jesus rises (still without a word), kisses him, and leaves.

Such, as Dostoyevsky saw them, were the temptations in the wilderness. Leaders willing to lie and accept men's surrender of freedom in return for tranquility, those who exercise the tyranny of tolerance, these Dostoyevsky the mystical artist, already in 1880, could foresee coming in the Marxist regime. We as Church must look deeply into our hearts. Do we see these temptations all around us? For example, do we understand media-generated permissiveness as a tyranny of tolerance? We must decide if we are able to accept the gift of freedom in Christ, already a subversive act in many cultures, and thus call people to their dignity and give them hope.

⚜

The Second Sunday of Lent, Cycle C
Genesis 15:5-12, 17-18; Philippians 3:17–4:1; Luke 9:28-36

When the Feast of the Transfiguration is celebrated on August 6, the Preface of the Mass accents the fact that Jesus' glorious body is the source and promise of our own glorification: "His glory shone from a body like our own, to show that the Church which is the Body of Christ would one day share his glory." In order to deepen our understanding of this we will concentrate on the teaching of our second reading, from St. Paul's Letter to the Philippians.

Paul begins by placing before his readers two models, one to imitate and the other to avoid. He begins: "Join in imitating me, brothers, and keep your eyes fixed on those who live according to the pattern I gave you" (Phil 3:17). Paul does not say this out of any conceit but in order to give a concrete norm of conduct to those for whom he has pastoral care: that norm is either himself or others who walk according to the same "pattern." Always implied in this teaching is his exhortation to the Corinthians: "Be imitators of me, as I am of Christ" (1 Cor 11:1, RSV). A Christian leader ought to be a model of how to imitate Christ, who is always the model.

Conformity to the image of the Son of God is the goal

174

of God's call: "Those he foreknew, he foreordained to be conformed to the image of his Son" (Rom 8:29). This is the true meaning of the imitation of Christ. It is a process of transformation, brought about by the Holy Spirit, by which the mystery, the revelation of God's plan in the death and resurrection of Christ, is made present to generation after generation in the Body of Christ.

Before developing this theme, Paul turns his attention to those whom the Philippians should not imitate: "For many walk, as I often told you and now say it weeping, as enemies of the cross of Christ. The end is ruin, their god is their belly, and their glory is their shame. They think only of the things of earth" (Phil 3:18-19).

One can be an enemy of the cross of Christ in many ways. There are those who despise any show of weakness and try to amass as much power as possible, ignorant of the fact that "the word of the cross is folly to those who are perishing, but to us who are being saved it is the power of God.... For the foolishness of God is wiser than men, and the weakness of God is stronger than men" (1 Cor 1:18, 25, RSV).

There are also those who seek to justify themselves and bypass or ignore the work of God in the cross of Christ: "I do not nullify the grace of God; for if justification were through the law, then Christ died to no purpose" (Gal 2:21, RSV). In the same way one can take one's belly as a god and glory in shame by a life of constant self-indulgence or by seeking to find salvation in dietary observances and physical practices. In either case all the concentration is on this earth, and there is no understanding of the transcendent wonder of that to which God calls us. That is why Paul goes on to speak of the Christian life.

"For our citizenship is in heaven, from where we await a Savior, the Lord Jesus Christ, who will transform our lowly bodies, conformed to his glorious body, in keeping with the effective energy of his power to subject all things to himself" (Phil 3:20-21). There is already at work in us a power that will transform us, body and soul, forever. It is the power now found in the risen Christ and communicated to us by the Holy Spirit. For God loves our bodies so much that he gave us the Holy Spirit to dwell in us. Thus the Spirit may do for our bodies what our souls could never do, namely, give our bodies eternal life.

This transforming power is the source and goal of Christian moral behavior. We live as friends of the cross of Christ, not as its enemies, because we deeply desire that the power of the cross transform us, in our bodies, our emotions, and our spirit. This energy now resides in the glorious Christ, who has the power to "subject all things to himself." We are not orphans, left alone to fend for ourselves and try to please God on our own. The very life of God is in us. Leading a heavenly life, therefore, does not mean ignoring the values and struggles of this life but rather embracing and meeting them with a seriousness that appreciates their significance for eternity.

⚜

The Third Sunday of Lent, Cycle C
Exodus 3:1-8, 13-15; 1 Corinthians 10:1-6, 10-12; Luke 13:1-9

The three readings for this Sunday treat first Moses' vocation, then the experience of Israel in the desert as an instruction for us, and finally the need for repentance. We will take St.

Paul's exhortation seriously, "Whoever thinks he is standing secure should take care not to fall" (1 Cor 10:12). Our Lord's call to repentance, placed by the Church here on this Third Sunday of Lent, is a call to all of us to examine our lives and our hearts and turn from sin.

In order to appreciate the teaching of a gospel text, it is helpful to recognize that the Spirit-endowed teachers and leaders of the early communities transmitted the tradition about Jesus, orally and in writing, before this tradition was confided to the written text of the gospels. The deeds and sayings of Jesus were related in a certain set way so as to transmit the honest truth about Jesus and contribute to an understanding of his words and actions. The Gospel writers took up and modified this interpretation of Jesus' activity, showing us how these events continue to exist and have power in and through his glorified humanity. Thus, three levels in the transmission process can be distinguished. The *Catechism of the Catholic Church* (126) describes these levels as "the life and teaching of Jesus; the oral tradition; the written Gospels."

Applied to the narrative in today's gospel, we see that St. Luke tells us about Jesus' call to repentance not merely as an historical reminiscence but as an address to all of us *today*. The liturgy of today makes that call present when we are gathered with others at the Sunday Mass. Recall these words of the Vatican Council: "In the liturgy God speaks to his people, and Christ is still proclaiming his Gospel" ("The Constitution on the Sacred Liturgy," 33).

Our gospel passage has two parts. The first is a conversation between Jesus and "some people" regarding two recent tragedies, and the second is a parable concerning repentance. First, the conversation:

There were some present at that very time who told him of the Galileans whose blood Pilate had mingled with their sacrifices. And he answered them, "Do you think that these Galileans were worse sinners than all the other Galileans, because they suffered thus? I tell you, No; but unless you repent you will all likewise perish. Or those eighteen, upon whom the tower in Siloam fell and killed them, do you think that they were worse offenders than all the others who dwelt in Jerusalem? I tell you, No; but unless you repent you will all likewise perish."

LUKE 13:1-5, RSV

It may be that the original interlocutors told Jesus about the Galileans killed by Pilate in order to see how Jesus, a Galilean himself, might react. Jesus immediately addresses himself to an underlying presupposition that there must have been something "wrong" with those Galileans to have met such a fate. "No, unless you repent you will all perish as they did." The word *repent*, especially as St. Luke uses it, means a turning from sin in order to accept the gift of salvation being presented in the preaching of Jesus and his disciples. It is not enough to be embarrassed by our sin; we must turn away from it and receive what the Lord is offering to us.

Jesus moves the conversation from the Galileans who were killed by Pilate to those who were killed by the accidental collapse of a tower in Jerusalem. He wants to make his point: we cannot see in such events a punishment of God upon those who particularly deserve it. "Do you think that they were worse offenders than all the others who dwelt in Jerusalem?" Again, in exactly the same words we hear the call to repentance.

In the second part of St. Luke's text we have a parable of

Jesus that is most likely included here to help us (the readers of another generation) to understand that God is still waiting for *our* repentance:

> A man had a fig tree planted in his vineyard; and he came seeking fruit on it and found none. And he said to the vinedresser, "Lo, these three years I have come seeking fruit on this fig tree, and I find none. Cut it down; why should it use up the ground?" And he answered him, "Let it alone, sir, this year also, till I dig about it and put on manure. And if it bears fruit next year, well and good; but if not, you can cut it down."
>
> LUKE 13:6-9, RSV

Listen to these words; let them resound in your heart. These are the words of Jesus Christ still proclaiming his gospel, to you, today. Is God inviting you to turn from sin of some sort and accept the gift of salvation?

※

The Fourth Sunday of Lent, Cycle C
Joshua 5:9-12; 2 Corinthians 5:17-21; Luke 15:1-3, 11-32

Our Lord's parable in the gospel today, that of the generous father and the prodigal son, is also proclaimed on the Saturday of the second week of Lent (see p.64) and you can refer back to that reading. Today we will reflect briefly on St. Paul's message concerning the transforming effects of being reconciled to God.

To speak of someone being "reconciled" implies a former

state of enmity, and this is precisely Paul's view of the effect of Jesus' death: "For, if when we were enemies, we were reconciled to God through the death of his Son, how much more, now reconciled, will we be saved by his life" (Rom 5:10, RSV). It is important to notice that the enmity was on our side: *we* were the enemies. In fact, never in the New Testament is it said that God was *reconciled,* it is always *he who is doing the reconciling,* bringing us back into friendship with himself. But there is more. In the death of Christ, the whole state of alienation that existed in both the physical or cosmic world and the world of human relations was healed. We have only to accept this to make it an ever more present reality. It is important to note this twofold extension of Christ's reconciling activity in the following passage from the Letter to the Colossians:

For in him all the fullness of God was pleased to dwell, and through him *to reconcile to himself all things,* whether on earth or in heaven, making peace by the blood of his cross. And you, who once were estranged and hostile in mind, doing evil deeds, he has now *reconciled in his body of flesh by his death,* in order to present you holy and blameless and irreproachable before him.

COLOSSIANS 1:19-22, RSV

In our passage today, Paul begins with a proclamation that when, through faith, God has placed us "in Christ," a profound and objective change takes place in us: "Therefore, if any one is in Christ, he is a new creation; the old has passed away, behold, the new has come" (2 Cor 5:17, RSV). We are already meant to be, in both body and spirit, part of the new universe that God is creating and whose model is the risen Christ. The language that Paul uses to express this mystery is that of reconciliation: "All this is from God, who through Christ reconciled us to himself and gave us the ministry of reconciliation; that is, in Christ, God was reconciling the world to himself, not counting their trespasses against them, and entrusting to us the message of reconciliation" (2 Cor 5:18-19, RSV).

Paul is not the agent of this reconciliation; God the Father has brought it about. Paul is rather its minister and preacher. It is, however, important to notice how urgent is this call to us to be reconciled. It has been accomplished in the death of Christ, but it must become a reality in the realm of our relation to God and to each other on the individual, gender, racial, social, and national levels: "So we are ambassadors for Christ, God making his appeal through us. We beseech you on behalf of Christ, be reconciled to God" (2 Cor 5:20, RSV).

The exhortation concludes with a daring statement: namely, that God made his own Son a sin offering, that he is thus in some way identified with sin, so that we, in our status as a new creation, might be identified with the righteousness of God: "For our sake he made him to be sin who knew no sin, so that in him we might become the righteousness of God" (2 Cor 5:21, RSV). If you wish to make this fact a reality in your own life, then listen to the Word of God: "We beseech you on behalf of Christ, be reconciled to God."

The Fifth Sunday of Lent, Cycle C
Isaiah 43:16-21; Philippians 3:8-14; John 8:1-11

The gospel for today, the story of the woman taken in adultery, is the same as that for tomorrow. For a meditation on the text see Monday of the fifth week, p. 105. Here we will concentrate our attention on the second reading, which embodies St. Paul's witness to his new life in Christ as he writes to his favorite community, the Christians at Philippi.

Paul has been warning his friends about those who claim that Jewish observances are necessary for a life of righteousness and that their right to teach others derives from their Jewish origin. For Paul, this is to have "confidence in the flesh." He goes on to assert that, on this basis, his own credentials are impeccable: "If any other man thinks he has reason for confidence in the flesh, I have more: circumcised on the eighth day, of the people of Israel, of the tribe of Benjamin, a Hebrew born of Hebrews; as to the law a Pharisee, as to zeal a persecutor of the church, as to righteousness under the law blameless" (Phil 3:4-6, RSV).

All of this was precious to Paul, yet in the light of his experience of Christ, it counts for nothing:

> But whatever gain I had, I counted as loss for the sake of Christ. Indeed I count everything as loss because of the surpassing worth of knowing Christ Jesus my Lord. For his sake I have suffered the loss of all things, and count them as refuse, in order that I may gain Christ and be found in him, not having a righteousness of my own, based on law, but that which is through faith in Christ, the righteousness from God that depends on faith.
>
> PHILIPPIANS 3:7-9, RSV

In these sentences Paul is making two points: first, that nothing can compare with knowing "Christ Jesus my Lord," and secondly, that this union with Christ comes about through faith, which is itself a gift of God and not the result of any human action or contrivance.

Finally, Paul opens his heart to the Philippians and to us: "So that I might know him, and the power of his resurrection, and sharing of his sufferings being conformed to his death, if somehow I might arrive at Resurrection from the dead" (Phil 3:9-10, RSV). The power of the resurrection is the power "in us the believers" (Eph 1:19), the power that is "made perfect in weakness" (2 Cor 12:9). We experience this power when we share the sufferings of Christ and are conformed to his death.

The knowledge that comes from this sharing in Christ's sufferings and being conformed to his death is so precious that the saints willingly forsook everything in order to lay hold of it—or rather to allow that knowledge to lay hold of them. The heart of this conformity lies in a trust in the Father, an ability to see his hand in the midst of suffering. Jesus trusted the Father right through death. We can know him with profound intimacy if we, too, will entrust ourselves to the Father even when we suffer. We never do a perfect job of this. There is always fear, reluctance, and even rebellion. But if we continue to look to the Father and identify our wills with that of Jesus, we will know an indescribable closeness to him that cannot be taken away from us.

Here Paul is our model as well. He quite honestly tells the Philippians that he is far from all that he wishes to be for God:

Not that I have already received all this, or that I am already perfect. I press on so that I might lay hold of it as I have been laid hold of by Christ Jesus. Brothers and sisters, I do not consider myself to have laid hold of it, but one thing: forgetting the things that are behind, stretching out for those that lie ahead, I press on toward the goal, for the prize of God's calling on high in Christ Jesus.

PHILIPPIANS 3:12-14

May these words encourage us to be faithful to God during this Lent.

⚜

Palm Sunday of the Lord's Passion, Cycle C
The Passion According to Luke, Luke 22:14–23:56

During cycles A, B, and C, the Church on this day reads the account of Our Lord's passion according to Matthew, Mark, and Luke respectively. We will concentrate on Jesus' teaching on discipleship as Luke records it in his Last Supper narrative. Luke places the teaching here so that we may understand that devotion to the Passion of Jesus is not complete unless it matures into humble service and confidence in Jesus' promise of an eternal life with him.

Jesus has just given himself, his Body and Blood, to the disciples at the Last Supper. He has just predicted that he will be betrayed, and the disciples begin to debate among themselves who would do such a thing. Then,

> a dispute broke out among them, who among them would seem to be the greatest? He said to them, "The kings of the pagans exercise lordship over them; and those in authority over them let themselves be called benefactors. With you, however, it shall not be so. Rather let the greatest among you be as the youngest, and the leader as one who serves. For who is the greater, one who sits at table or one who serves? Is it not the one who sits at table? But I am among you as one who serves.
>
> LUKE 22:24-27

184

Jesus first paints a portrait of the power games of the world. Those with money, connections, and inherited positions of power impose themselves on the others, who connive in the game in order to survive. This whole view of life depends upon equating authority—considered a necessary evil at best—with power, and power with the ability to impress yourself and your will upon others. In this situation of domination and fawning connivance, titles are forged and attributed to the "great ones."

Jesus reverses this fundamental law of human relating in a world scarred by sin. "With you, however, things will not be so." The greatest now is to be as "powerless" as the youngest in the group. It is not by fear that he maintains his position but by love. That is why the leader is the one who serves.

With these words, and their parallels in Matthew and Mark, Jesus is not merely redefining social roles. He is pointing to what may be called a Messianic family, in which identity, security, and future are found in the community of believers: "My mother and my brothers are those who hear the word of God and do it" (Lk 8:21, RSV). There is leadership but not domination; there may be rank but it does not carry privilege. Someone may object that this is excessively idealistic, but this is to ignore two essentials of Christian living: first, the example of Jesus himself and his ability to enable us to imitate him; second, the fact that our true center of gravity is union with Jesus in his suffering and future glory.

Jesus addresses the first of these: "For who is the greater, one who sits at table or one who serves? Is it not the one who sits at table? But I am among you as one who serves." Luke probably intends these words to refer back to the Eucharist and to the Passion which underlies it. There we will find our motivation and the ability to live out the meaning of the Eucharist in imitation of Jesus' self-giving service. The Eucharist is not a ceremony. It is a sacrament: the sacrament of the Lord's death and resurrection.

The second essential of Christian living follows immediately in Luke's text: "You are those who have continued with me in my trials; and I confer kingship upon you, as my Father conferred kingship upon me, that you may eat and drink at my table in my kingdom, and sit on thrones judging the twelve tribes of Israel" (Lk 22:28-30). The second principle of Christian leadership is that disciples are to continue with Jesus in his trials. This was addressed to the immediate disciples, but Luke records it here as applicable to all future generations, as is the rest of the statement. Those who suffer with Jesus will share his royal authority and will enjoy the fulfillment of the Eucharistic banquet in the heavenly banquet, where we will rejoice with him and sit with him in glory: "I will give the victor the right to sit with me on my throne, as I myself was victorious and sit down with my Father on his throne" (Rv 3:21).

Today we honor the victory of Jesus. We look to him as our Savior who will enable us to imitate him as servant and feast with him at his banquet.

⚜

The Easter Vigil, Cycle C
Luke 24:1-12

The only difference among the Vigil liturgies of various cycles has to do with the gospel of the Resurrection. In cycle C the account is taken from St. Luke's Gospel, which has in common with the other two narratives the mention of the women who go to anoint the body of Jesus, the discovery of the empty tomb, the proclamation by a "young man" (in Mark) or angel(s) (in Matthew and Luke) of the Resurrection. We will meditate particularly on the proclamation as it is found in Luke.

> But on the first day of the week, at early dawn, they [the women] went to the tomb, taking the spices which they had prepared. And they found the stone rolled away from the tomb, but when they went in they did not find the body. While they were perplexed about this, behold, two men stood by them in dazzling apparel; and as they were frightened and bowed their faces to the ground, the men said to them, "Why do you seek the living among the dead? Remember how he told you, while he was still in Galilee, that the Son of man must be delivered into the hands of sinful men, and be crucified, and on the third day rise." And they remembered his words, and returning from the tomb they told all this to the eleven and to all the rest.

LUKE 24:1-9, RSV

The heart of this proclamation includes the announcement that Jesus is living and that "the Son of man *must* be delivered into the hands of sinful men, and be crucified, and on the third day rise." On the way to Emmaus Jesus explains to the two crestfallen disciples: "*Must not* the Messiah have suffered these things and enter his glory?" (Lk 24:26). And again, later in the evening, Jesus speaks with the disciples back in Jerusalem:

"These are my words which I spoke to you, while I was still with you, that everything written about me in the law of Moses and the prophets and the psalms *must* be fulfilled." Then he opened their minds to understand the scriptures, and said to them, "Thus it is written, that the Christ should suffer and on the third day rise from the dead, and that repentance and forgiveness of sins should be preached in his name to all nations, beginning from Jerusalem. You are witnesses of these things."

LUKE 24:44-48, RSV

Why *must* the Messiah suffer, die, and rise? Certainly there is nothing intrinsic in the order of the universe that dictates such a thing. The necessity comes from the will of the Father. As the angels tell the women, and as Jesus points out to the two on the way to Emmaus and to the group in Jerusalem, this will of the Father can already be discerned in "Moses, the prophets, and the psalms."

God does not change. The incarnation, death, and resurrection of the Second Person of the Trinity was decided upon from all eternity. In this unfathomable mystery of the love between the Father and the Son and the Holy Spirit, the plan was always understood that the Son would come to our rescue. We can hardly lift the veil on this mystery.

Still, it is important to realize that God can "adjust" himself to our free will without any impairment of his own freedom. We can see that in our own lives. How many times have we willfully done what was not what God wanted of us, and yet God has guided our lives and brought us to him? In the same way the sin of the first parents, and the sin of all the rest of us throughout history, was known to God from all eternity, and yet neither our freedom nor God's is thereby diminished. Yes, it is true, the Messiah had to suffer and enter his glory, but that necessity comes purely from the infinite freedom and love of God.

This is the mystery that the angels can scarcely look into. The fire of love that burns between the Father and the Son spills out into our world, surrounding our freedom and inviting us to return to the light. Now the risen Jesus, the Incarnate Son of God, has become our life and our salvation. Come to the banquet, come to the victory celebration, come and be filled with the mercy of God—that exceeds our capacity to imagine.

I pray that he give to you, in keeping with the riches of his glory, to be strengthened with power through his Spirit unto the inner man; that Christ dwell, through faith, in your hearts, rooted and grounded in love; so that you may be strong enough to comprehend, with all the saints, what [is] the width and length and height and depth; thus to know the love of Christ surpassing knowledge, that you may be filled unto all the Fullness of God. Amen.

EPHESIANS 3:16-19

CHAPTER TEN

The Two Major Feasts in Lent Honoring Joseph and Mary

There are two important feasts that are always celebrated during Lent. They are the Feast of St. Joseph and the Feast of the Annunciation. The first of these has been in the liturgical calendar since the twelfth century and has achieved progressively greater importance in the life of the Church. The moment of the Incarnation has been the object of a special feast since the seventh century. In a special way it honors Mary, whose *fiat* was the threshold for the entrance of the Word into the very fabric of human history.

❧

The Feast of Saint Joseph, Husband of Mary, March 19

2 Samuel 7:4-5, 12-14, 16; Romans 4:13, 16-18, 22;
Matthew 1:16, 18-21, 24

All the texts today reflect the fact that, in the Incarnation, God himself became part of a family and through his belonging to this family became part of the human race. Jesus was not only born of a woman, of a special woman in a special way, he was born into a family, that of Mary and Joseph. In Jesus, too, was realized the saying of Pope John Paul II, "All of humanity passes through the family." The human identity of the Son of God is expressed by calling him "the son of Mary," and in regard to descent and family appurtenance, "the son of Joseph."

We honor today the man who has been called "the shadow of the Father." Although he was not the physical father of Jesus, who was born of the virgin, Mary, he exercised the role of a human father in Jesus' life. Thus Jesus entered society known as the son of Joseph: "When Jesus began his ministry he was about thirty years old, the son, it was thought, of Joseph son of Heli" (Lk 3:23). Those who knew Jesus must have seen the love and respect he had for Joseph. Not only, therefore, is Joseph the reason why Jesus is legally a descendant of David, but Jesus' very demeanor must have let people see how authentically he related to Joseph as to a father.

The same mystery of the human ancestry of Jesus is recalled in St. Paul's list for the Romans of the privileges of Israel: "They are Israelites, and to them belong the sonship, the glory, the covenants, the giving of the law, the worship, and the promises; to them belong the patriarchs, and of their race, according to the flesh, is the Christ" (Rom 9:4-5, RSV). Based on this thinking, Luke, in his genealogy of Jesus, traces his lineage up through Abraham to Adam. Matthew, on the other hand, gives us "the genealogy of Jesus Christ, son of David, son of Abraham," naming the two ancestors of Jesus to whom a special promise was made concerning their posterity. These are the two men who figure in the first two liturgical readings for today.

The Second Book of Samuel tells us how David, looking at his palace, compared it with the tent that still housed the ark of the covenant. He resolved to build a dwelling worthy of the Lord. Nathan, his prophet and "spiritual director," approved of the plan, but "that night the word of the Lord came to Nathan." In effect, the Lord told David, "You will not build me a house; I will build you a house, the House of David. And while son after son will succeed to your throne, One will come who will be Son of David. In a unique way, I will be his Father, and he will be my Son. He will build a temple for me that will be his very body."

In the second reading St. Paul holds up Abraham, whose act of faith in God's promise of posterity allowed God to make him "the father of many nations." Through this one man's seed all the nations of the earth would be blessed. This seed is Christ, "the son of David, the son of Abraham." Joseph is the means by which this descendancy from Abraham and David is established, so that Jesus is the Son "who was descended from David according to the flesh and designated Son of God in power according to the Spirit of holiness by his resurrection from the dead" (Rom 1:3-4, RSV).

Finally, in the gospel we hear how St. Joseph received his vocation to be on earth "the shadow of the Father." Before they lived together, Mary was found to be with child through the Holy Spirit. Joseph, her husband, "being a just man and unwilling to put her to public shame, resolved to divorce her quietly." Most likely, Joseph did not want to take as his own an offspring that he suspected was of God. That is why the angel said to him: "Joseph, son of David, do not fear to take Mary as your wife, for that which is conceived in her is of the Holy Spirit; she will bear a son, and you shall call his name Jesus, for he will save his people from their sins."

This just man was given his vocation: to take Mary as his wife and to begin his role as father to Jesus by naming him. Though Mary and Joseph did not have conjugal relations, theirs was a real marriage. As Thomas Aquinas points out, they had a deep and permanent commitment to each other, and their marriage was fruitful in a Child.[1]

All of these themes are beautifully summed up in the Preface for this feast, which says of Joseph: "He was that just man, that wise and loyal servant, whom you placed at the head of your family. With a husband's love he cherished Mary, the virgin Mother of God. With fatherly care he watched over Jesus Christ your Son, conceived by the power of the Holy Spirit."[2]

Let us pray today for all Christian families and for the fathers in these families, that they be just, wise, and loyal, cherishing their wives and watching over their children with fatherly care.

The Annunciation of the Lord, March 25
Isaiah 7:10-14, 8:10; Hebrews 10:4-10; Luke 1:26-38

Today we celebrate the mystery of the Incarnation. The first two readings are dedicated to the theme of the bodily reality of Jesus, the Son of God, and the implications of this for human history. The gospel recalls God's invitation to Mary to be the mother of his Son, the human being who says yes to God in the name of us all.

In the text from Isaiah we hear of the Lord's Word to Ahaz. The kings of Aram and Israel have combined to attack Jerusalem, dethrone Ahaz, and put a foreigner, who thus interrupts David's line, in his place. The passage tells us that the heart of both king and people "trembled as the trees of the forest tremble in the wind." Isaiah tells Ahaz to ask God for a sign, but Ahaz refuses, saying that he does not want to tempt the Lord. In actuality a sign would oblige him even more to trust in God, and that he is unwilling to do.

Nevertheless, Isaiah gives him the sign. First he alludes to the promise made to David by addressing the word to the "house of David," and then he gives the sign: "Hear then, O house of David! Is it too little for you to weary men, that you weary my God also? Therefore the Lord himself will give you a sign. Behold, the virgin shall conceive and bear a son, and shall call his name Emmanuel (which means 'God is with us')" (Is 7:13-14, RSV).

This sign, as it was directed to Ahaz, concerns the queen mother, who will conceive and bear a son, thus ensuring the endurance of the promise made to David that one of his own descendants would always be on the throne. Isaiah, at the end of his life, or perhaps a disciple, clearly saw that the prophecy about "God with us" stretched far into the future and concerned a future Son of David. Matthew saw this and said of the announcement to Joseph of the birth of Jesus, "All this took place to fulfill what the Lord had spoken by the prophet: 'Behold, the virgin shall conceive and bear a son, and they shall call his name Emmanuel (which means, God with us)'" (Mt 1:22-23, RSV).

In a significant change from Isaiah's prophecy, Matthew tells us that "they," that is, all the people rather than the mother alone, will call this child Emmanuel, "God with us." At the other end of his Gospel he has these words of Jesus himself, "Behold, *I am with you always* until the end of the age." In other words, every day of our lives, and throughout all history, the Church is meant to know the truth and fulfillment of this prophecy: Christ is with us.

The gospel today tells us of God's invitation to Mary to become the mother of his Son. God, after all, was not looking for a surrogate womb but for a *mother;* thus her free consent was necessary. Let us reflect on these words from Pope John Paul II's Apostolic Letter *On the Dignity and Vocation of Women* (4).

Thus the "fullness of time" manifests the extraordinary dignity of the "woman." On the one hand, this dignity consists in the supernatural elevation to union with God in Jesus Christ, which determines the ultimate finality of the existence of every person both on earth and in eternity. From this point of view, the "woman" is the representative and the archetype of the whole human race: she represents the humanity which belongs to all human beings, both men and women. On the other hand, however, the event at Nazareth highlights a form of union with the living God which can only belong to the "woman," Mary: the union between mother and son....
At the moment of the Annunciation, by responding with her "fiat," Mary conceived a man who was the Son of God, of one substance with the Father. Therefore she is truly the Mother of God, because motherhood concerns the whole person, not just the body, nor even just human "nature." In this way the name "Theotokos"—Mother of God—became the name proper to the union with God granted to the Virgin Mary....
At the same time, however, through her response of faith Mary exercises her free will and thus fully shares with her personal and feminine "I" in the event of the Incarnation. With her "fiat," Mary becomes the authentic subject of that union with God, which was realized in

the mystery of the Incarnation of the Word, who is of one substance with the Father. All of God's action in human history at all times respects the free will of the human "I." And such was the case with the Annunciation at Nazareth.

Only Mary is the Mother of God. However, there is a way in which she conceived the Word in her mind, by a loving reception of him, long before she conceived him in her body. In this sense, we are all called to be a mother to Christ, to conceive him in our heart and to bear him to the world: "Whoever does the will of God is brother and sister and mother to me" (Mk 3:35, RSV).

AFTERWORD

We have celebrated the Paschal Mystery. Now, during the next fifty days, we rejoice in the presence of the Holy Spirit as we listen to the readings from the Acts of the Apostles describing the ongoing life of Christ in the Church, a life made present by the action of the Holy Spirit. The gospel readings are taken from the Gospel of John. They are meant to instruct us about the work of the Holy Spirit in the midst of the Church and within each believer. We will hear about being born of water and the Holy Spirit in chapter three of John's Gospel, we will be instructed about the "spiritual eating" of the Eucharistic bread in chapter six, and we will read once again the five solemn promises of Jesus concerning the coming Paraclete (Jn 14:15-17, 25-26, 15:26-27; 16:7-11; 16:12-15).

On the feast of Pentecost we will celebrate the other dimension of the same Paschal Mystery, namely, that activity of the Holy Spirit who makes alive and accessible all that Jesus accomplished. We pray in the Fourth Canon: "And that we might live no longer for ourselves but for him, he sent the Holy Spirit from you, Father, as his first gift to those who believe, to complete his work on earth and bring us the fulness of grace." All of our Lenten preparation and all of our celebration of Holy Week and Easter were done in the power and life-giving action of the Holy Spirit. Now we stop and recognize the presence and activity of him who was given to the Church at that moment when Jesus "handed over the Spirit"

(Jn 19:30), confirmed by the Lord when he breathed on his disciples in the Upper Room after the Resurrection, and made manifest to the world at Pentecost. As Pope John Paul II teaches us in his Encyclical, *The Holy Spirit in the Life of the Church* (#25),

> What had then taken place inside the Upper Room, "the doors being shut", later, on the day of Pentecost is manifested also outside, in public. The doors of the Upper Room are opened and the Apostles go to the inhabitants and the pilgrims who had gathered in Jerusalem on the occasion of the feast, in order to bear witness to Christ in the power of the Holy Spirit.

In the same paragraph, the Holy Father quotes Vatican II's *Constitution on the Church* (#4) to describe the various activities of the Holy Spirit in the Church:

> As the Council writes, "the Spirit dwells in the Church and in the hearts of the faithful as in a temple (cf. 1 Cor 3:16; 6:19). In them he prays and bears witness to the fact that they are adopted sons (cf. Gal 4:6; Rom 8:15-16, 26). The Spirit guides the Church into the fullness of truth (cf. Jn 16:13) and gives her a unity of fellowship and service. He furnishes and directs her with various gifts, both hierarchical and charismatic, and adorns her with the fruits of his grace (cf. Eph 4:11-12; 1 Cor 12:4; Gal 5:22). By the power of the Gospel he makes the Church grow, perpetually renews her, and leads her to perfect union with her Spouse."

Lord Jesus Christ, when the Father raised you to his right hand, he gave to you the promised Holy Spirit, and you poured him out on the Church. We celebrate the glory of your resurrection and ask you to send down upon us and upon the whole Church the Holy Spirit from the Father to transform us and bring us into conformity with your death and resurrection. When the world sees that we have put aside our divisions and enmities, that we have yielded to your Spirit and obey your command to care for those who need care, that our marriages and homes are places of peace, and that we praise you with a full heart, then it will have hope and accept the invitation to believe.

NOTES

Introduction

1. St. Augustine, *Confessions*, 7, 10, 16.
2. John Paul II, *On the Coming of the Third Millenium*, 10.
3. St. Leo, *On the Passion*, 12 (Sources Chrétiennes, 74, 82).
4. Corpus Christianorum Latinorum, Series Medievalis 9, 231.
5. Columba Marmion, *Christ in His Mysteries*, Mother M. St. Thomas, trans. (London: Sands & Co., 1939), 22–24.

Chapter Three
The Second Week of Lent

1. Kieran Kavanaugh, O.C.D., and Otilio Rodriguez, O.C.D., trans., *The Collected Works of St. Teresa of Avila, Vol. 1* (Washington, D.C.: ICS, 1976), 6.3.

Chapter Four
The Third Week of Lent

1. *Rite of Christian Initiation of Adults*, International Committee on English in the Liturgy (ICEL) and National Conference of Catholic Bishops (NCCB) (Chicago: Liturgy Training Publications, 1988), 141, 144.
2. *Rite of Christian Initiation of Adults*, 85.

Chapter Five
The Fourth Week of Lent

1. Adapted from the scrutiny of the Fourth Sunday of Lent, *Rite of Christian Initiation of Adults, Study Edition* (Chicago: Liturgy Training Editions, 1988), 99.
2. From *The Roman Missal*, International Committee on English in the Liturgy.
3. From the Easter Proclamation.

Chapter Six
The Fifth Week of Lent

1. Karol Wojtyla (John Paul II), *The Theology of the Body. Human Love in the Divine Plan. L'Osservatore Romano*, trans. (Boston: Pauline, 1997), 242.
2. *Rite of Christian Initiation of Adults*, 107.
3. Catherine of Siena, *The Dialogue*, 25 Suzanne Noffke, trans. (New York: Paulist, 1980), 63.

Chapter Seven
Holy Week and Easter

1. *The Liturgy of the Hours* (New York: Catholic Book Publishing Co., 1976), 2:497–98.
2. Francis Martin, *Touching God* (Denville, N.J.: Dimension, 1975), 79–80.
3. Martin, *Touching God*, 7.

Chapter Nine
The Sundays of Lent, Cycle C

1. Lines in italics are taken directly from Fyodor Dostoyevsky, *The Brothers Karamasov,* David Margashack, trans. (New York: Penguin, 1984).

Chapter Ten
The Two Major Feasts in Lent

1. St. Thomas Aquinas, *Summa Theologiae* 3, 29, 2.
2. From the Roman Missal, translated by the International Committee on English in the Liturgy.